101 THINGS TO MAKE

FUN CRAFT PROJECTS WITH EVERYDAY MATERIALS

JULIET BAWDEN
Illustrated by Alex Pang

Sterling Publishing Co., Inc.   New York

CONTENTS

3   Paper, Print and Paint

Design by David West Children's Book Design

Illustrated by Alex Pang

Library of Congress Cataloging-in-Publication Data

Bawden, Juliet,
    101 things to make: fun craft projects with everyday materials/by
  Juliet Bawden: illustrated by Alex Pang.
      p.   cm.
    Includes index.
    ISBN 0–8069–0596–4
    1. Handicraft—Juvenile literature.   2. Models and modelmaking
  —Juvenile literature.   3. Textile crafts—Juvenile literature.
  4. Paperwork—Juvenile literature.   (1. Handicraft.   2. Models and
  modelmaking.   3. Textile crafts.   4. Paper work.) I. Pang, Alex, ill.
  II. Title.   III. Title: One hundred one things to make. IV. Title:
  One hundred and one things to make.
  TT180.B337   1993   93–29633
  746.5—dc20   CIP
                                                 AC

10 9 8 7 6 5 4 3 2 1

Published 1994 by Sterling Publishing Company, Inc.
387 Park Avenue South, New York, N.Y. 10016
Originally published in Great Britain by
Simon & Schuster Young Books Ltd
Text © 1991 by Juliet Bawden
Illustrations © 1991 by Simon & Schuster Young Books
Distributed in Canada by Sterling Publishing
% Canadian Manda Group, P.O. Box 920, Station U
Toronto, Ontario, Canada M8Z 5P9

Printed and bound in Hong Kong

Sterling ISBN 0–8069–0596–4

1
Models

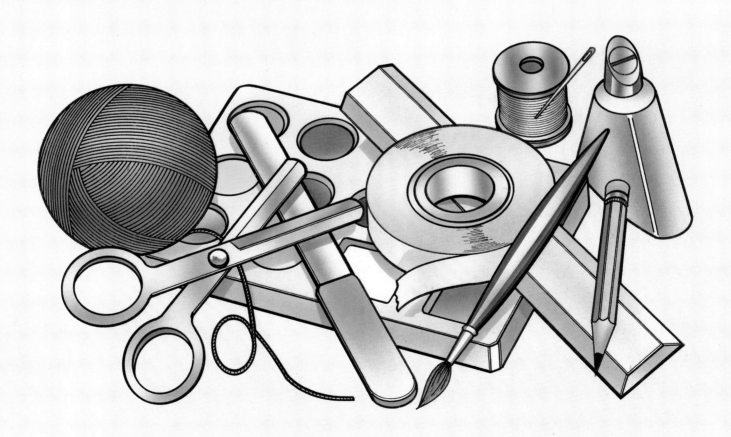

INTRODUCTION

The purpose of this section is to introduce the techniques of modeling, forming and casting. The ideas are intended to fire your imagination so that once you have mastered the basics you can then go on to experiment and create your own designs. There are lots more ideas at the back of this section.

All the materials used in this book are easy to find and fairly cheap. Many of the objects can be made from things found around the home. Almost everything else can be bought from your nearest craft shop.

Before you start:

* Wear an apron or old shirt to protect your clothing.
* Read all the instructions carefully.
* Collect all the materials and equipment together that you will need.
* Cover work surfaces with plenty of newspaper to protect them. Give yourself plenty of room to work.
* When using knives, make sure that you have a board underneath.
* Keep modeling materials such as clay, Fimo or salt dough in a plastic bag to stop them drying out.
* CLEAN UP after yourself.
* Look out for this sign ⊕ throughout the instructions. It means "be careful."

MATERIALS AND TOOLS

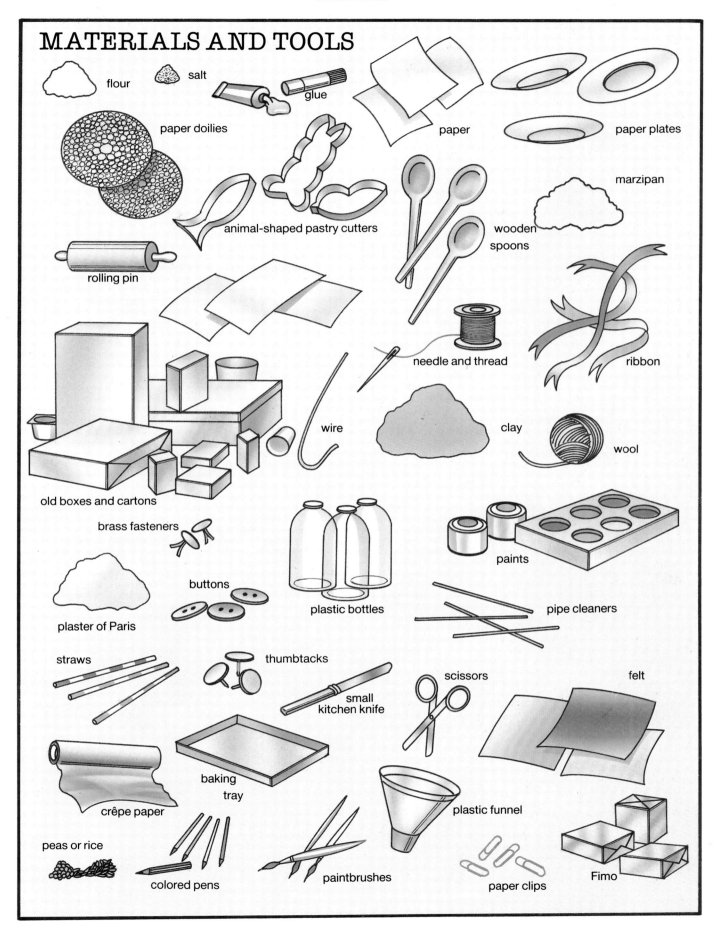

flour

salt

glue

paper doilies

paper

paper plates

animal-shaped pastry cutters

marzipan

wooden spoons

rolling pin

needle and thread

ribbon

wire

clay

wool

old boxes and cartons

brass fasteners

paints

plaster of Paris

buttons

plastic bottles

pipe cleaners

straws

thumbtacks

scissors

felt

small kitchen knife

crêpe paper

baking tray

plastic funnel

peas or rice

colored pens

paintbrushes

paper clips

Fimo

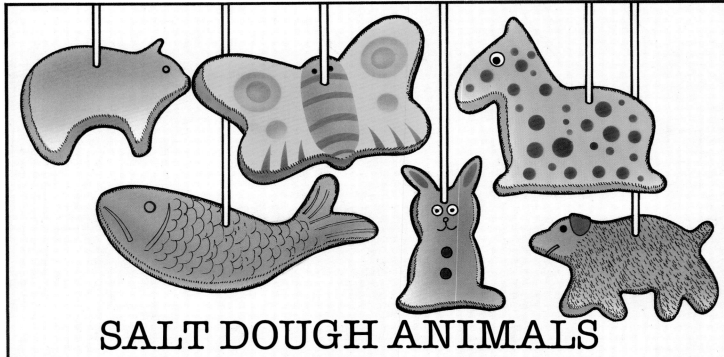

SALT DOUGH ANIMALS

What you need

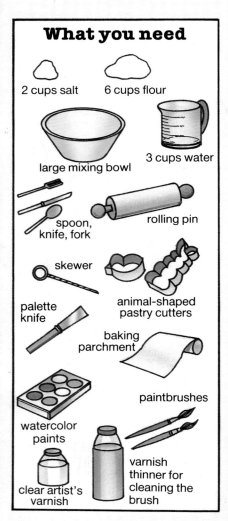

2 cups salt

6 cups flour

large mixing bowl

3 cups water

spoon, knife, fork

rolling pin

skewer

palette knife

animal-shaped pastry cutters

baking parchment

paintbrushes

watercolor paints

clear artist's varnish

varnish thinner for cleaning the brush

1 Heat the oven to 300°F.

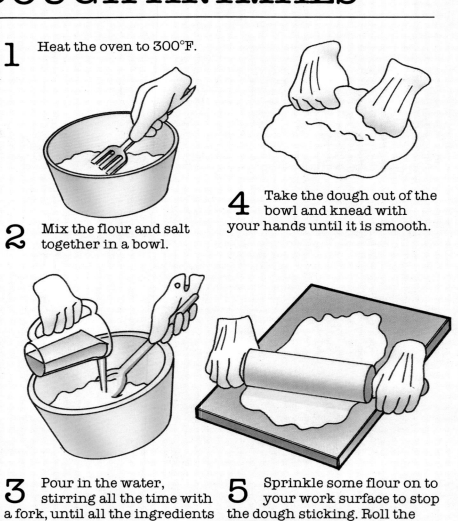

2 Mix the flour and salt together in a bowl.

3 Pour in the water, stirring all the time with a fork, until all the ingredients form a dough.

4 Take the dough out of the bowl and knead with your hands until it is smooth.

5 Sprinkle some flour on to your work surface to stop the dough sticking. Roll the dough flat with the rolling pin.

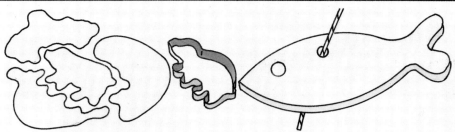

6 Using the pastry cutters, cut out animal shapes.

7 Using a skewer, make holes for the eyes and mouth.

8 With the leftover dough, roll thin sausages with your fingers and stick these on for wool, horns, hair etc.

9 Use a knife to mark feathers on a chick, or the back of a spoon to mark the scales on a fish. A fork can make a rough woolly coat.

10 Make a hole, for hanging the animal, using a skewer.

11 Lift the shape, using a palette knife, on to the baking parchment which you have put on the baking tray.

12 Place in the oven and bake until hard and golden brown. This can take between two and four hours. ⊕

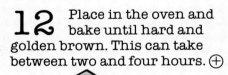

13 When the animals are cool, paint them with watercolor paints.

14 When the paint is dry, varnish the animals on the front and sides and leave to dry. Then varnish the back and leave to dry.

15 Hang up the animal shapes to decorate your Christmas tree. Hang from ribbons to make a necklace or attach a brooch fastening on the back.

WOODEN SPOON PUPPETS

What you need

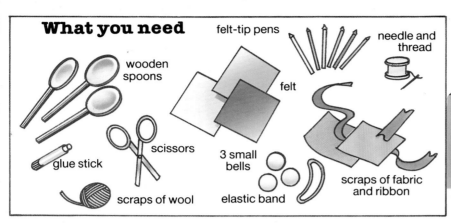

felt-tip pens

wooden spoons

felt

needle and thread

glue stick

scissors

3 small bells

elastic band

scraps of fabric and ribbon

scraps of wool

HOBBY HORSE

1 Place the wooden spoon on top of a piece of felt and draw around the top of the spoon. Move the spoon along and draw around it again.

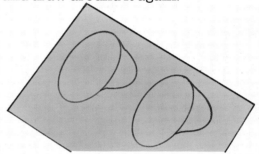

2 Draw a horse's head around these shapes and cut it out. Repeat on another piece of felt.

3 Turn these shapes over and stick them together with the spoon in between.

4 Make eyes, a bridle and reins with felt and stick them on.

SALLY SPOON

1 Draw a face on the back of a large wooden spoon.

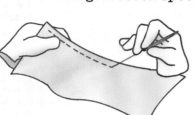

2 To make a skirt, cut a piece of fabric approximately 1in wide and 4in long, and sew a line of running stitch along the top.

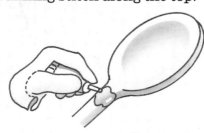

3 Put some glue around the handle where you want to attach the top of the skirt.

4 Gather up the running stitches and wrap the material around the handle of the spoon.

5 Tie a piece of ribbon round the gathers.

6 Draw shoes and socks on the bottom of the handle.

7 You can draw on hair, or cut some strands of wool and tie another piece of wool around the center of this bundle. Glue onto the top of the spoon. If you wish to make bunches, tie with ribbons.

JOLLY JESTER

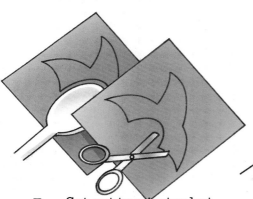

1 Cut out two jester hat shapes from felt, making sure that the brim of the hat will fit on top of your spoon.

2 Glue the shapes together, with the bottom edges on either side of the top of the spoon.

3 Cut out eyes, nose, rosy cheeks and mouth from felt and stick them on to the back of the spoon.

4 Sew small bells to the three points of the hat.

5 Wind an elastic band around the neck of the spoon until it is tight and then tie different colored ribbons or scraps of fabric to the elastic.

BRILLIANT BEADS, BADGES AND BUTTONS

What you need

- Fimo (in different colors)
- thin knitting needle
- plastic knife
- paintbrush
- piece of card
- clear artist's varnish
- paints
- coins
- safety pins
- needle and thread
- rolling pin
- chopping board
- varnish thinner for cleaning the brush

All the beads, badges and buttons are made from Fimo. See page 36 for instructions on working with Fimo.

BEADS

1 Roll a piece of Fimo into a long, even sausage shape about ³⁄₈in thick with your fingers.

2 Cut it into ³⁄₈in sections.

3 Mold the beads into balls, squares or rectangles, or squash them to make a flat bead.

4 Add your own decoration by pricking with a pin, or adding more pieces of Fimo in different colors.

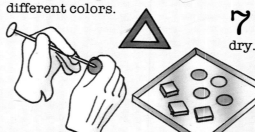

5 Make a hole through the center of each bead with a thin knitting needle.

6 Bake the beads following the instructions on the Fimo packaging. ⊕

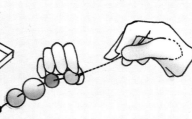

7 When cool, coat the beads with varnish and leave to dry.

8 Thread a needle with a double thickness of cotton, tying a knot at one end, and string the beads on to the thread to make necklaces and bracelets.

BADGES

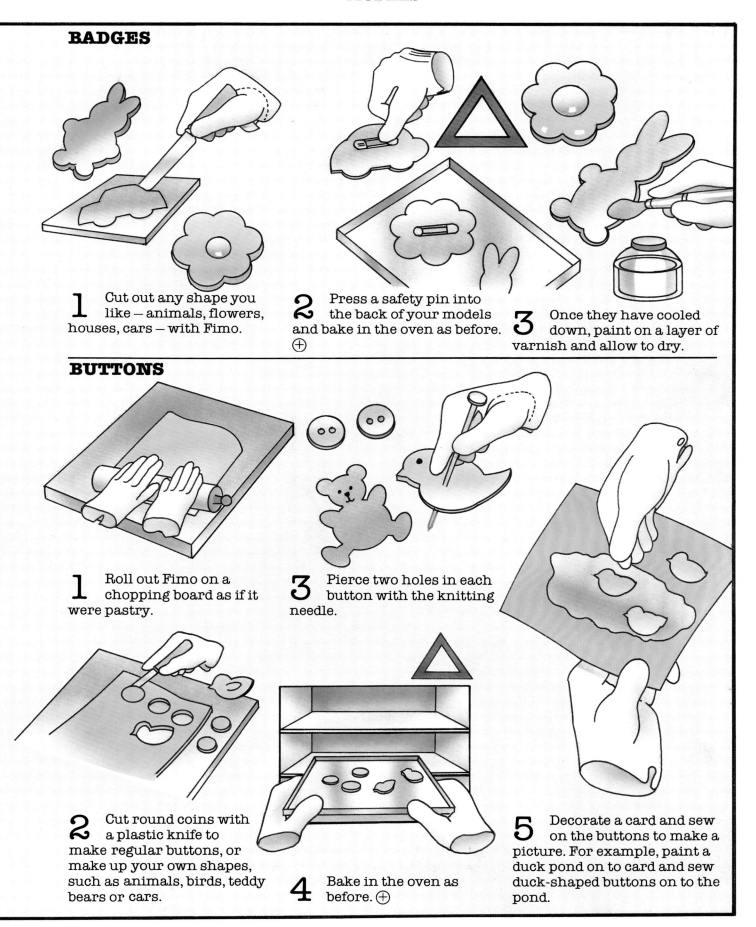

1 Cut out any shape you like – animals, flowers, houses, cars – with Fimo.

2 Press a safety pin into the back of your models and bake in the oven as before. ⊕

3 Once they have cooled down, paint on a layer of varnish and allow to dry.

BUTTONS

1 Roll out Fimo on a chopping board as if it were pastry.

3 Pierce two holes in each button with the knitting needle.

2 Cut round coins with a plastic knife to make regular buttons, or make up your own shapes, such as animals, birds, teddy bears or cars.

4 Bake in the oven as before. ⊕

5 Decorate a card and sew on the buttons to make a picture. For example, paint a duck pond on to card and sew duck-shaped buttons on to the pond.

ANIMALS FROM BOXES

What you need

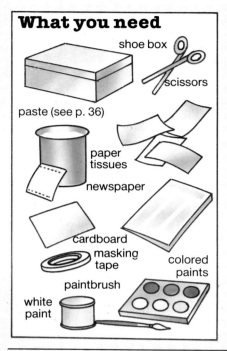

shoe box

scissors

paste (see p. 36)

paper tissues

newspaper

cardboard

masking tape

colored paints

paintbrush

white paint

This box is made with Papier Mâché. See page 36 for instructions on working with Papier Mâché. You can use different-shaped boxes to make all sorts of animals — a tiger, a caterpillar, a snake or a badger.

CROC-A-BOX

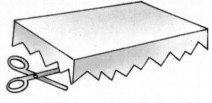

1 Cut zigzags around three sides of the top of the box.

2 Mix the paste according to the instructions on p. 36.

3 Dip wads of tissue into the paste and stick them over the lid of the box. Leave to dry.

4 Cut out a mouth with teeth shape on the front of the bottom of the box.

5 Stick wads of tissue, dipped in the paste, over the two long sides of the box and halfway up the back of the box. Leave to dry.

6 From cardboard, cut two eye shapes and one nose shape.

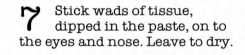

7 Stick wads of tissue, dipped in the paste, on to the eyes and nose. Leave to dry.

8 Rip up ³⁄₈in-wide strips of newspaper, dip them into the paste and pass between your thumb and forefinger to get rid of any excess paste.

14

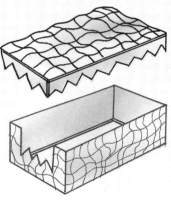

9 Cover the lid and the box with the strips of newspaper.

10 When one layer is finished, leave it to dry and then do another layer, until there are six layers. This is Papier Mâché.

11 Cover the eyes and nose with Papier Mâché. Leave to dry.

12 Make two slits in the lid and fit the eyes into them. If they won't stand up, secure them underneath with masking tape.

13 Tape the nose into position.

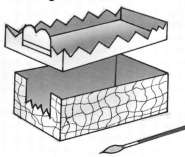

14 Paint the inside of the box and lid red.

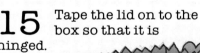

15 Tape the lid on to the box so that it is hinged.

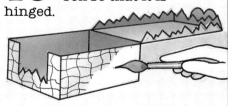

16 Paint the outside of the box white. When this paint is dry, paint over with green paint.

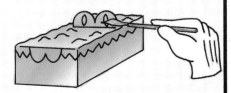

17 Paint eyes and holes for the nose.

MINIATURE HOUSE

What you need

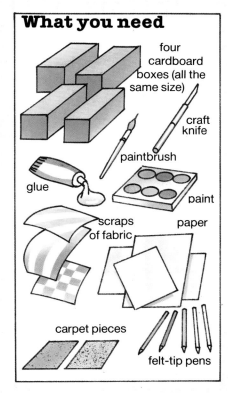

four cardboard boxes (all the same size)

craft knife

paintbrush

glue

paint

scraps of fabric

paper

carpet pieces

felt-tip pens

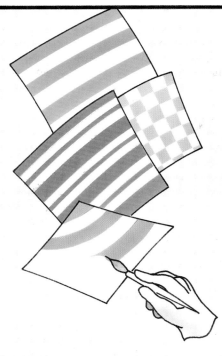

5 You can make different floor coverings for each room. Draw floorboards with brown felt-tip pens. Make carpets with fabric scraps or real carpet pieces.

3 Paint patterns on your paper to make wallpaper for each of the four rooms.

HOUSE

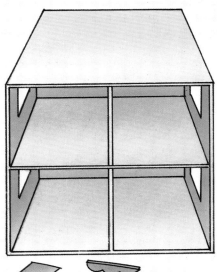

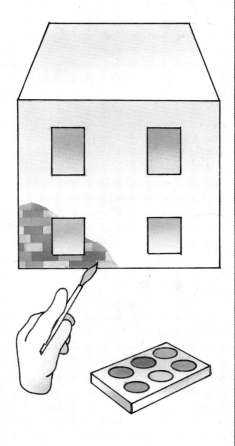

1 Make a house by gluing the four cardboard boxes together to form a square, with the openings to the front.

2 Cut out windows and add curtains or blinds.

4 Stick the paper in the different rooms.

6 Paint the outside of the house. You could paint on bricks or even beams.

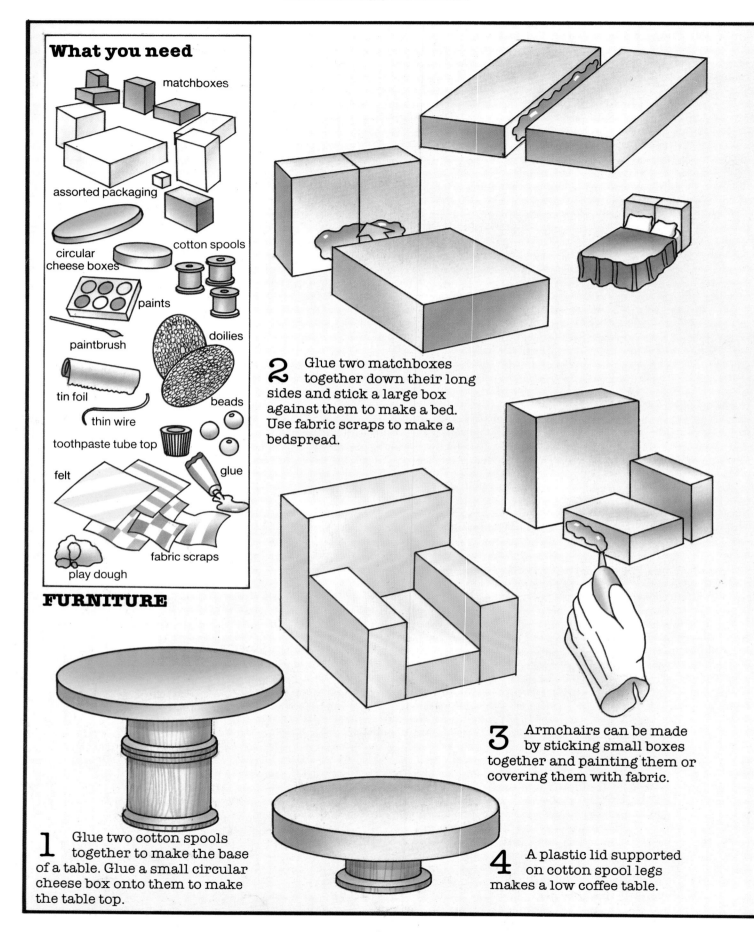

What you need

matchboxes

assorted packaging

circular cheese boxes

cotton spools

paints

paintbrush

doilies

tin foil

beads

thin wire

toothpaste tube top

felt

glue

play dough

fabric scraps

FURNITURE

2 Glue two matchboxes together down their long sides and stick a large box against them to make a bed. Use fabric scraps to make a bedspread.

3 Armchairs can be made by sticking small boxes together and painting them or covering them with fabric.

1 Glue two cotton spools together to make the base of a table. Glue a small circular cheese box onto them to make the table top.

4 A plastic lid supported on cotton spool legs makes a low coffee table.

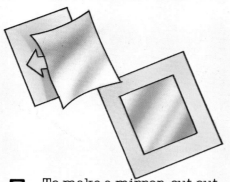

5 To make a mirror, cut out a rectangle of tin foil and stick it onto cardboard. Cut it out, leaving a slightly larger rectangle of cardboard around it as a frame, and stick it on the wall.

6 Matchboxes stacked one on top of the other with beads as handles make miniature chests of drawers.

7 Paint tiny pictures and frame them with bits of doily to decorate the walls.

8 To make a pot of flowers, glue tiny pieces of felt onto the ends of thin wire. Stick these into play dough in a toothpaste tube top.

What you need

pipe cleaners

cotton

buttons with large holes

embroidery thread

fabric scraps

PIPE CLEANER PEOPLE

1 Twist a pipe cleaner to make the head and arms.

2 Turn a button upside down and thread another pipe cleaner through it. Hook the ends of the pipe cleaner over the arms.

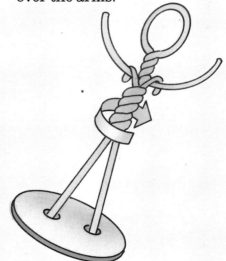

3 Twist to make the body.

4 Wedge a bit of cotton in the top loop to make the face, and wind the embroidery thread around the body.

5 Make clothes and scarves from fabric scraps.

PAPER PLATE MASKS

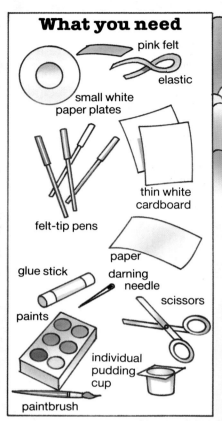

What you need

pink felt

elastic

small white paper plates

thin white cardboard

felt-tip pens

paper

glue stick

darning needle

paints

scissors

individual pudding cup

paintbrush

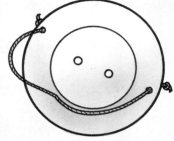

1 Hold the paper plate up to your face, bottom side out.

2 Ask a friend to mark where the eyes, mouth and nose are with a pen. Cut holes for them.

3 Cut a piece of elastic 8in long, thread it onto a darning needle and knot one end.

4 Make a hole ⅜in in from the side of the plate and thread the elastic through. Take the elastic through to the other side of the plate and thread it through another hole ⅜in from the edge. Remove the needle and knot this end of the elastic.

1 Repeat steps 1–4.

2 Paint the plate pink.

3 Make the ears out of pink felt and stick on.

4 Squash an individual pudding cup, paint it pink and stick it on for the nose.

5 Draw the mouth with a felt-tip pen.

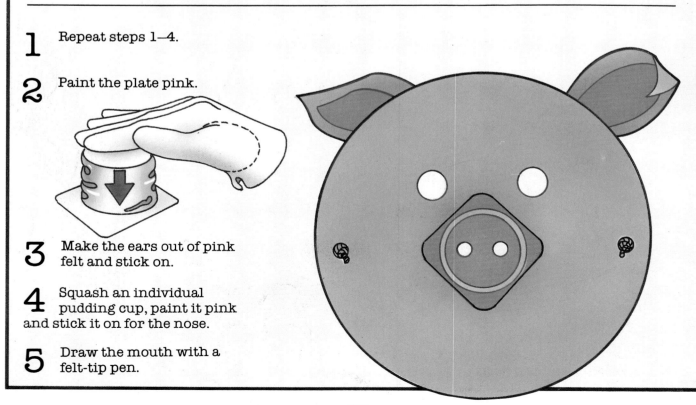

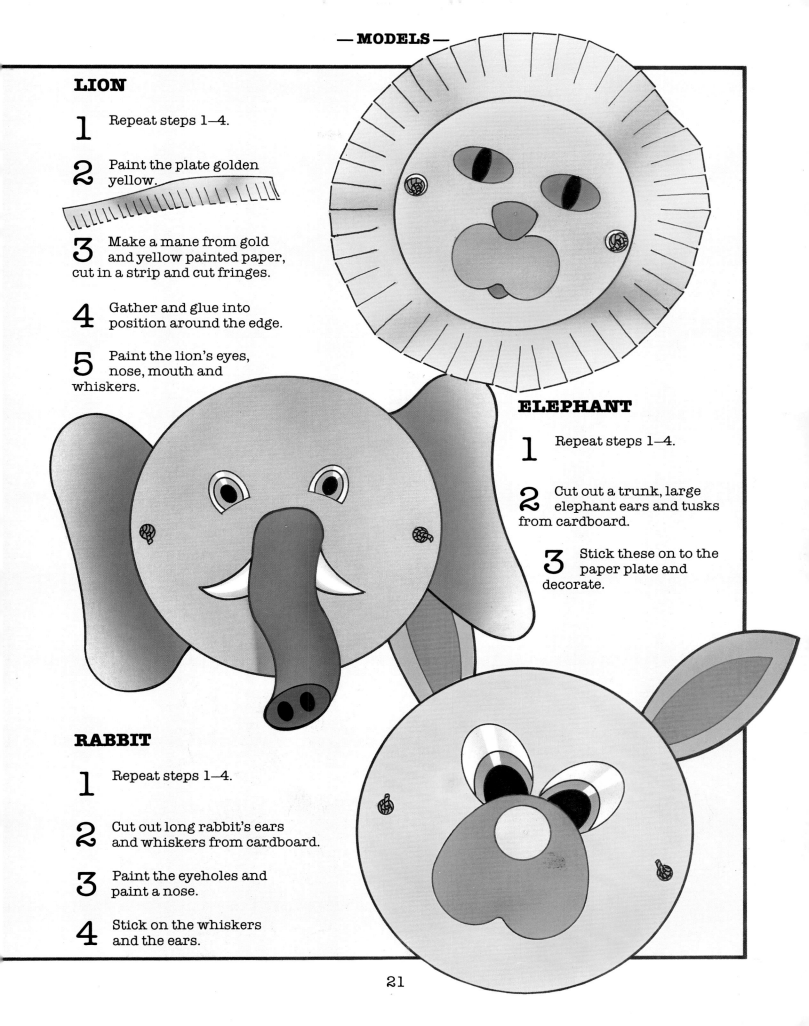

LION

1 Repeat steps 1—4.

2 Paint the plate golden yellow.

3 Make a mane from gold and yellow painted paper, cut in a strip and cut fringes.

4 Gather and glue into position around the edge.

5 Paint the lion's eyes, nose, mouth and whiskers.

ELEPHANT

1 Repeat steps 1—4.

2 Cut out a trunk, large elephant ears and tusks from cardboard.

3 Stick these on to the paper plate and decorate.

RABBIT

1 Repeat steps 1—4.

2 Cut out long rabbit's ears and whiskers from cardboard.

3 Paint the eyeholes and paint a nose.

4 Stick on the whiskers and the ears.

21

WINDMILL

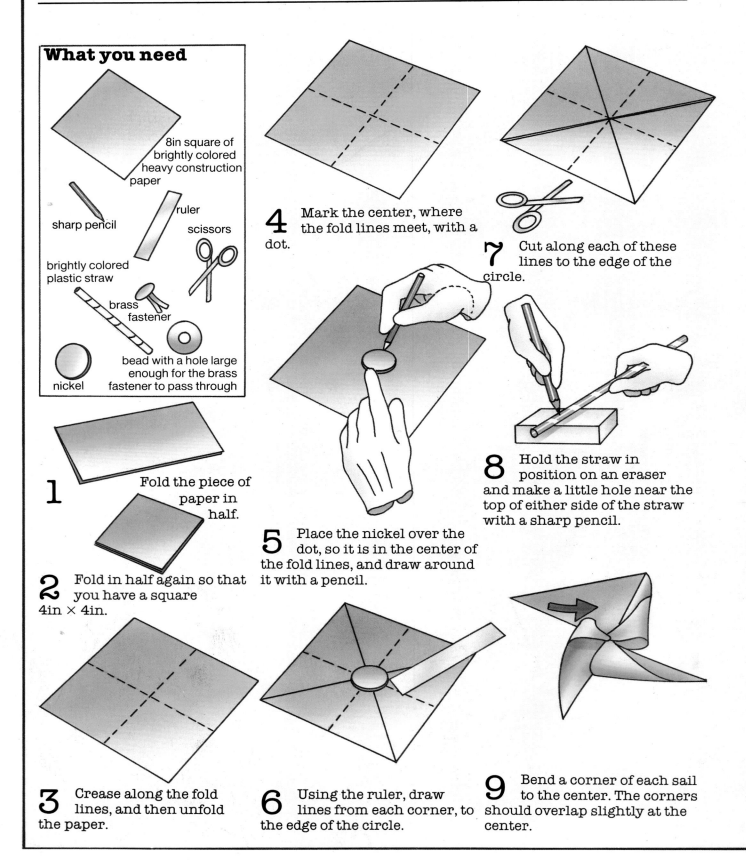

What you need

8in square of brightly colored heavy construction paper

sharp pencil

ruler

scissors

brightly colored plastic straw

brass fastener

bead with a hole large enough for the brass fastener to pass through

nickel

1 Fold the piece of paper in half.

2 Fold in half again so that you have a square 4in × 4in.

3 Crease along the fold lines, and then unfold the paper.

4 Mark the center, where the fold lines meet, with a dot.

5 Place the nickel over the dot, so it is in the center of the fold lines, and draw around it with a pencil.

6 Using the ruler, draw lines from each corner, to the edge of the circle.

7 Cut along each of these lines to the edge of the circle.

8 Hold the straw in position on an eraser and make a little hole near the top of either side of the straw with a sharp pencil.

9 Bend a corner of each sail to the center. The corners should overlap slightly at the center.

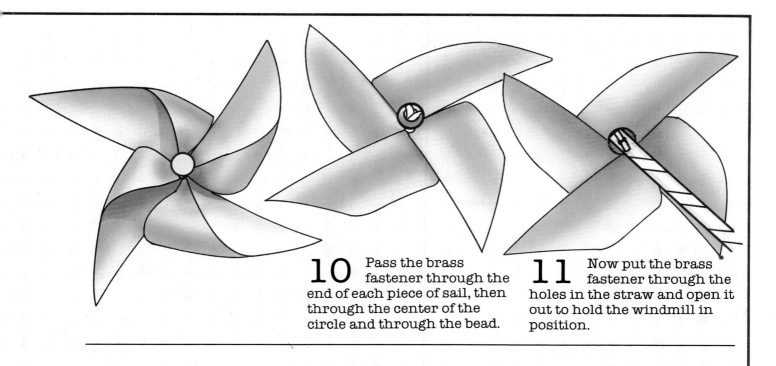

10 Pass the brass fastener through the end of each piece of sail, then through the center of the circle and through the bead.

11 Now put the brass fastener through the holes in the straw and open it out to hold the windmill in position.

ARMOR

See page 36 for information on working with Papier Mâché. From this one method you can make all different kinds of masks and helmets.

What you need

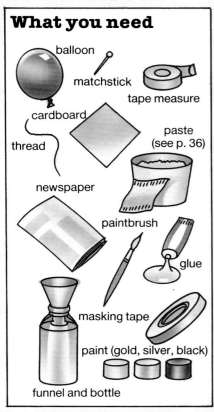

balloon
matchstick
tape measure
cardboard
paste
(see p. 36)
thread
newspaper
paintbrush
glue
masking tape
paint (gold, silver, black)
funnel and bottle

PAPIER MÂCHÉ HELMET

1 Measure the circumference of your head with the tape measure.

2 Blow up the balloon to slightly larger than this measurement.

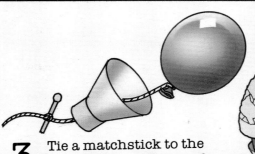

3 Tie a matchstick to the thread. Pass one end of the thread through the funnel and tie the other to the balloon. The matchstick will keep the balloon in place while you work.

4 Tape the funnel to the bottle.

5 Mix up the paste according to the instructions on page 36.

6 Rip the newspaper into strips. Dip in the paste and lay in overlapping strips over the balloon until its top half is completely covered. Leave to dry.

7 Repeat step 6 five more times, until you have a thick strong helmet shape.

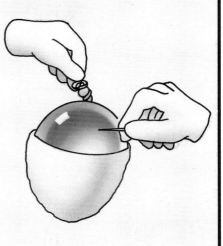

8 Remove the balloon from the funnel and bottle and prick the balloon.

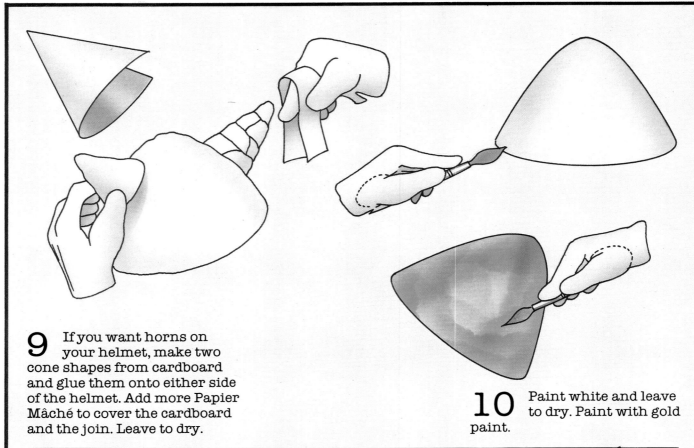

9 If you want horns on your helmet, make two cone shapes from cardboard and glue them onto either side of the helmet. Add more Papier Mâché to cover the cardboard and the join. Leave to dry.

10 Paint white and leave to dry. Paint with gold paint.

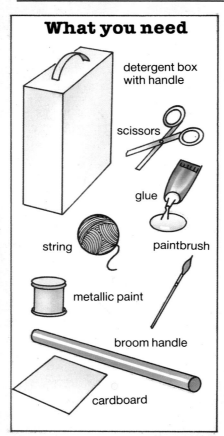

What you need

detergent box with handle

scissors

glue

string

paintbrush

metallic paint

broom handle

cardboard

SHIELDS, SPEARS AND AXES

1 Cut off the front of the box. Keep the lid with the handle.

2 Draw the shape you want your shield to be and cut it out of the box front.

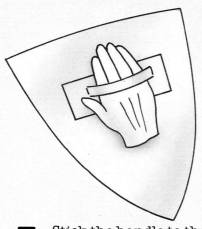

3 Stick the handle to the center back of the shield.

5 Paint with white paint, leave to dry, and then coat it in metallic paint.

7 Decorate with string and then paint as you did the shield.

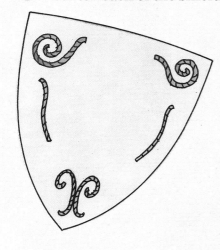

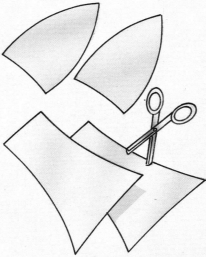

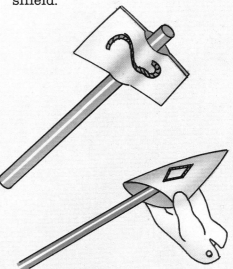

4 Decorate the front of the sheild by sticking the string on in patterns.

6 Make a spear or an axe by cutting out the spearhead or axehead shape in cardboard twice.

8 Glue the two sides together with a broom handle in between.

BOWLING

What you need

10 empty
plastic
soda
bottles

newspaper

paste (see p. 36)

poster or acrylic
paints

ball (sized
between a
tennis ball
and a small
soccer ball)

funnel

paintbrushes

clear artist's
varnish

filling (dried beans,
peas, rice)

matchstick

varnish thinner for
cleaning the brush

See page 36 for information on
working with Papier Mâché.

5 Rip the newspaper into
strips and cover with
paste. Stick the pieces of paper
on to the bottles, overlapping
slightly as you go, until every
bottle is completely covered
with one layer of paper. Leave
to dry.

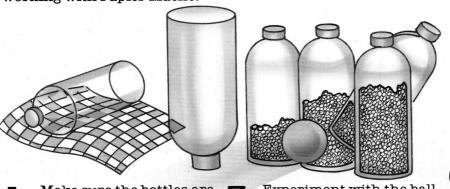

1 Make sure the bottles are
clean and totally dry
inside.

3 Experiment with the ball
and the filled bottles to
see if they fall down when hit.
If not, remove some of the
filling and try again before
beginning to Papier Mâché.

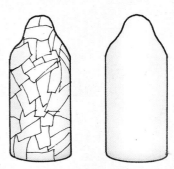

6 Repeat step 5 five more
times. Allow the Papier
Mâché to dry between layers.

7 When all the bottles have
had six layers of Papier
Mâché, paint each one white.

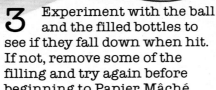

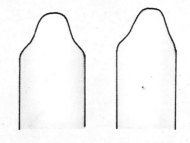

2 Take the cap off each
bottle and pour the filling
in through the funnel.

4 Mix the paste according
to the instructions on
page 36.

8 If the newsprint still
shows through when the
paint is dry, give them another
coat of white paint.

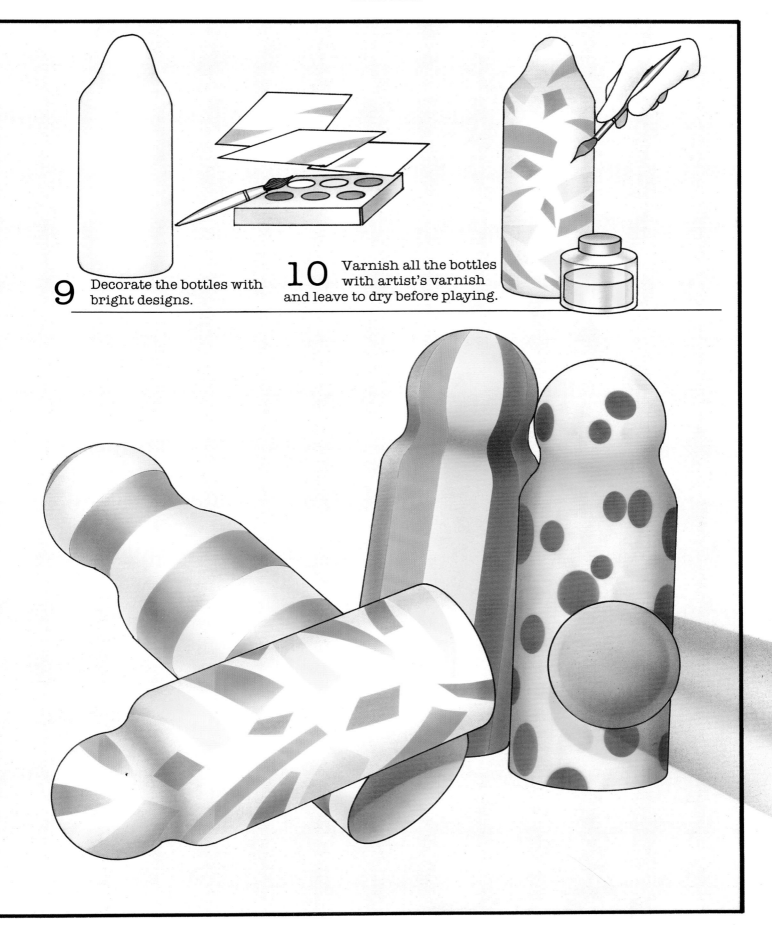

9 Decorate the bottles with bright designs.

10 Varnish all the bottles with artist's varnish and leave to dry before playing.

MARZIPAN MONSTERS

It's fun to make model monsters and even more fun when you can eat them!

What you need

4oz/½ cup confectioners' sugar

1 egg

8oz/2¼ cups ground almonds

4oz/1 cup superfine sugar

2 cups

1 lemon

lemon squeezer

food colorings

wooden spoon

chocolate drops

1 teaspoon almond flavoring

1 teaspoon vanilla

fork

vermicelli

bowl

new paintbrush or pastry brush

chocolate strands

1 Using a wooden spoon, mix the confectioners' sugar, superfine sugar and ground almonds in a bowl.

2 Break the egg into a cup and beat with a fork.

3 Using the lemon squeezer, squeeze the juice of a lemon and pour into another cup.

4 Mix the essences and the beaten egg with the dry mixture.

5 If the mixture is dry and crumbly add 1 or 2 teaspoons of lemon juice.

6 Form the marzipan into monster shapes. Make sausage shapes for snakes and antennae, balls and oval shapes for heads and bodies.

7 Paint the monsters with food coloring.

8 Use chocolate strands, vermicelli and chocolate drops to decorate the monsters.

PLASTER CASTING HANDS

What you need

clay

plaster of Paris

rolling pin

paints

paintbrush

See page 36 for instructions on working with plaster of Paris.

3 Roll out a sausage of clay and put it round the edge of the imprinted clay to build a wall.

4 Make sure the join is very strong and add more clay if there is any doubt whatsoever.

1 Roll out the clay so that it is large enough to cover your hands.

2 Press the backs, NOT the palms, of your hands into the clay so it makes an imprint. It will imprint your nails as well.

5 Mix the plaster and pour it onto the clay. Leave it to set.

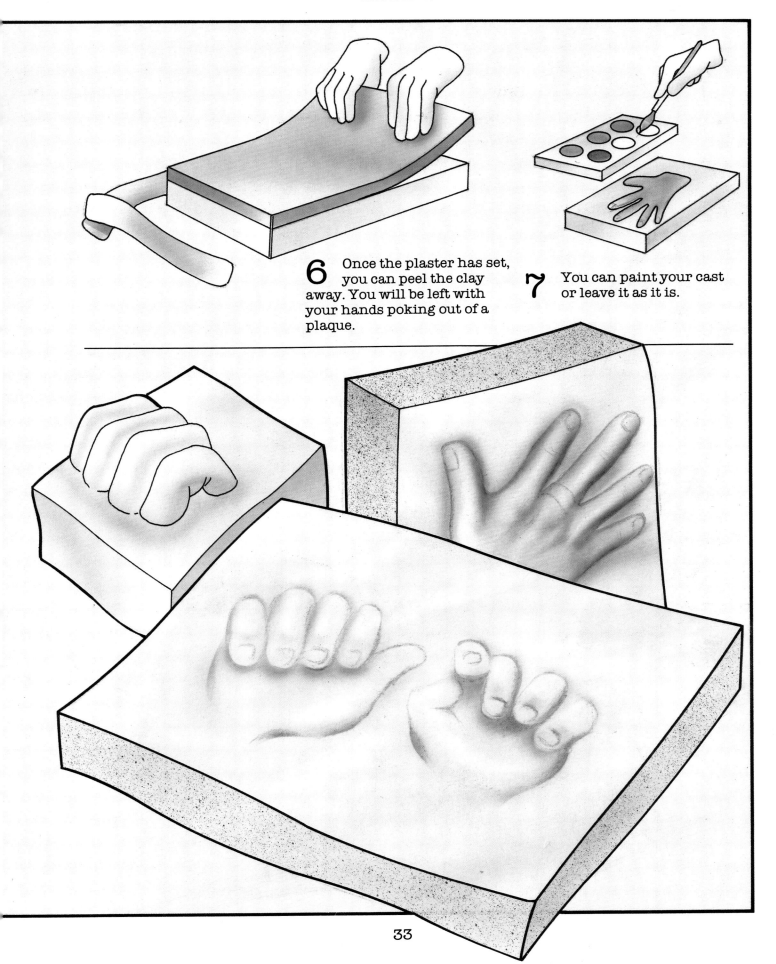

6 Once the plaster has set, you can peel the clay away. You will be left with your hands poking out of a plaque.

7 You can paint your cast or leave it as it is.

MORE IDEAS

SALT DOUGH (pages 8—9)

You can make many kinds of models from salt dough, including magnets, plaques, garlands, mobiles and Christmas decorations.

To make a nameplate for your bedroom door, roll out the dough and cut out an oval about 4½in across. Make thin sausages of dough with your fingers and push them into place to form your name.

WOODEN SPOONS (pages 10—11)

Paint the handles and wrap ribbons round the spoons to make them pretty. Paint on the name of the person to whom you wish to give the spoon.

FIMO (pages 12—13)

As well as beads, badges and buttons, Fimo can be used to make models, puppet heads, napkin rings, hat and tie pins, nameplates and all kinds of jewellery. To marble Fimo, roll out two thin sausages of different colours and twist them together. Roll this into a ball and knead.

PAPIER MÂCHÉ BOXES (pages 14—15)

These make wonderful presents, or packaging for gifts that you have already made or bought. They make pretty boxes for storing money, pencils, sewing thread, buttons or jewelry.

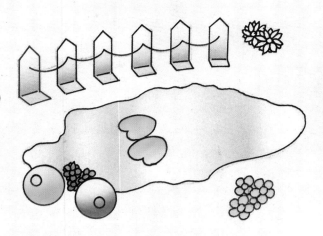

MAKING MINIATURES (pages 16—19)

Once you start thinking in miniature you can make all sorts of things as well as furniture. Decorate a model railway with fences, roads, a zebra crossing, benches, flowers, trees or a pond. You could make miniature equipment for a space station, a fort or a castle.

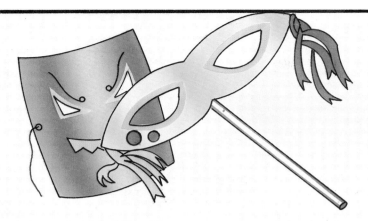

MASKS (pages 20—21)

Masks can be made from cardboard, paper bags, junk or Papier Mâché. They can be on sticks, hiding the eyes but revealing the rest of the face. They can be decorated with feathers or sequins. They may look beautiful, mysterious, frightening or funny.

BOWLING (pages 28—29)

Instead of filling bottles with dried beans, why not use sand and make a doorstop? Decorate the doorstop so it looks like a person.

WINDMILLS (pages 22—23)

Decorate your own paper before you make windmills. Fill a vase with brightly colored windmills to cheer up a room.

MARZIPAN MONSTERS (pages 30—31)

As well as monsters you could make teddy bears, fruits or animals from marzipan. These make excellent presents for grown-ups and children alike.

ARMOR (pages 24—27)

As well as armor, shields, spears and axes, you could also make epaulettes from cardboard and crêpe paper fringing. Cover buttons with milk bottle tops to make them look military. Make buckles from cardboard and cover with tin foil.

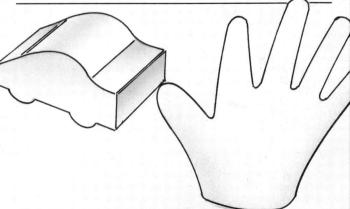

PLASTER CASTING (pages 32—33)

Caste a plain block of plaster and then carve out a shape from it. Fill a rubber glove with plaster and use it as a ring stand.

SPECIAL MATERIALS AND TECHNIQUES

FIMO

Fimo is a modeling clay which comes in a variety of colors. It needs to be squeezed and kneaded to make it soft and pliable. Always work on a clean surface so that the colors remain pure. Once opened, wrap individual colors in plastic wrap. Check that the baking temperatures on the colors are the same before using them together. Bake in the oven at the specified temperatures, until hard.

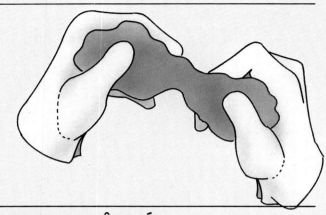

PAPIER MÂCHÉ

All you need to make Papier Mâché is paper and glue. The glue can be made from flour and water, in the proportions of 1 part of flour to 3 of water. Heat the flour and water together in a saucepan, stirring all the time, ⊕ then leave to cool before using. Alternatively you can use wallpaper paste. Rip the paper into strips and cover each piece with glue. Then stick the glued paper onto your mold. If you are using a mold which you will be using again, cover the mold with Vaseline or oil so that you can pull the Papier Mâché off once it is dry. Once you have covered your mold with one layer of paper, leave it to dry. Repeat until there are about six layers.

PLASTER OF PARIS

Plaster of Paris can be bought at most craft stores. You can cast anything three-dimensional from plaster of Paris, from coins and shells to your own hands and feet. Make a clay mold (see page 32). Measure the water into an old mixing bowl (use 1 unit of water to 2 of plaster). It is better to mix up too much plaster than too little. Add the plaster and, as soon as it starts to thicken, pour into your clay mold. While the plaster is in the mold, clean the bowl and spoon by scraping the plaster onto newspaper. Plaster of Paris begins to harden within two or three minutes, so you will have to work fast. Never put plaster of Paris down the sink or toilet, as you can block them!

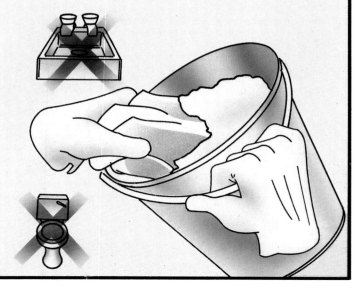

2

Textiles

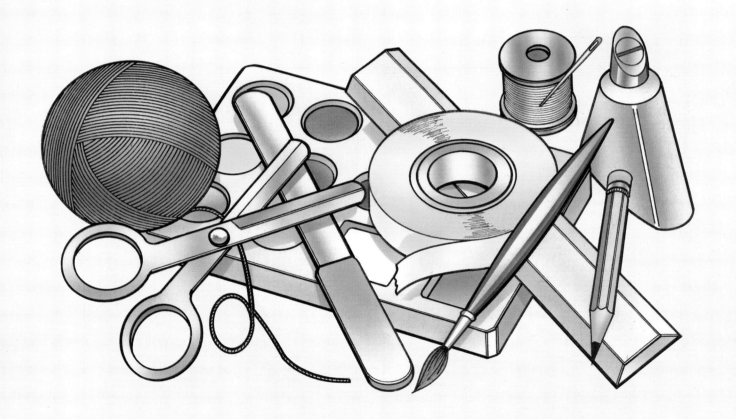

INTRODUCTION

This section introduces you to many activities involving textiles
and other materials. The techniques included are printing,
fabric painting, tie-dye, cross stitch, appliqué,
patchwork, weaving and cutting.
Many of the articles made in this section are
environmentally friendly and re-use materials.

Before you start:

* Read all the instructions carefully.
* Clear yourself a work space.
* Collect together all the materials and equipment you
  need.
* If you are printing or dyeing, wear an overall or an apron.
  It is a good idea to wear rubber gloves as well, as the dye
  or ink may stain your hands.
* Make sure that you do not drop scissors, needles or pins
  on the floor.
* Clean up after yourself.
* Look out for this sign ⊕ throughout the instructions. It
  means "be careful"!

MATERIALS AND TOOLS

plain and patterned fabric

glitter, puffy and plastic fabric paints

fabric pens

potatoes

vegetables

felt

yarn

sequins and beads

tacks

pencil and paper

string

cardboard

socks

wool

pebbles

dye and fixative

embroidery thread

cord

paintbrush

scissors

masking tape

pins

graph paper

needles

bucket and measuring cup

DECORATING T-SHIRTS

What you need

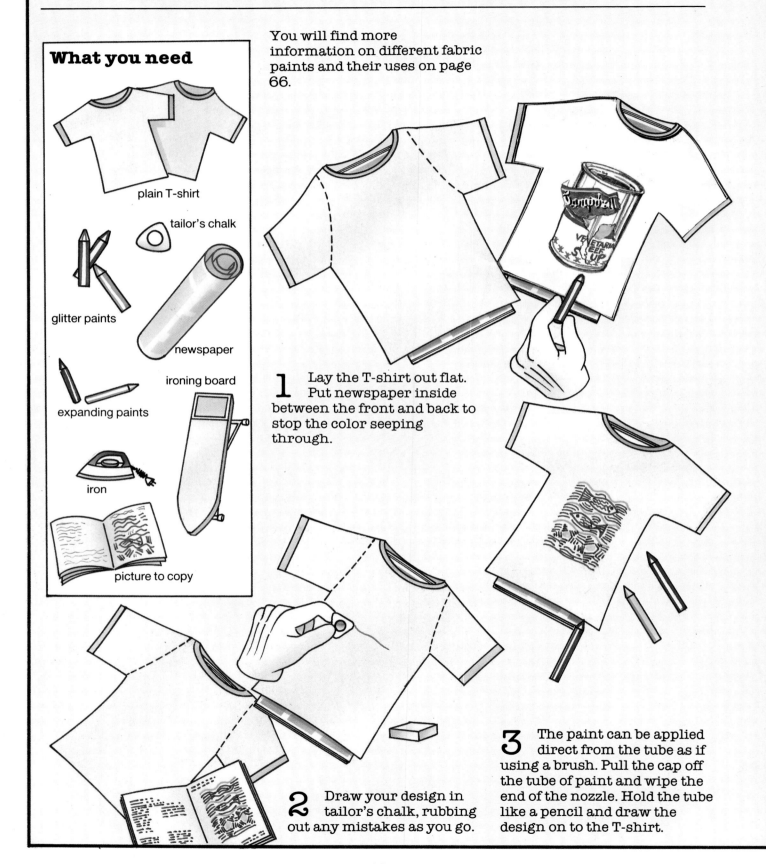

plain T-shirt

tailor's chalk

glitter paints

newspaper

expanding paints

ironing board

iron

picture to copy

You will find more information on different fabric paints and their uses on page 66.

1 Lay the T-shirt out flat. Put newspaper inside between the front and back to stop the color seeping through.

2 Draw your design in tailor's chalk, rubbing out any mistakes as you go.

3 The paint can be applied direct from the tube as if using a brush. Pull the cap off the tube of paint and wipe the end of the nozzle. Hold the tube like a pencil and draw the design on to the T-shirt.

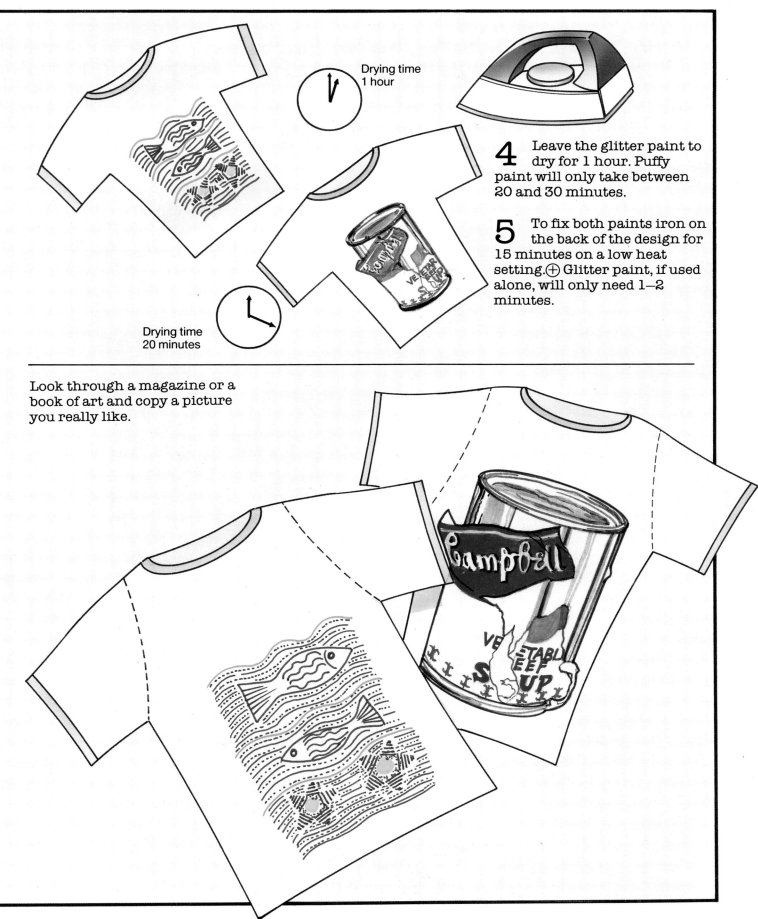

Drying time
1 hour

4 Leave the glitter paint to dry for 1 hour. Puffy paint will only take between 20 and 30 minutes.

5 To fix both paints iron on the back of the design for 15 minutes on a low heat setting.⊕ Glitter paint, if used alone, will only need 1–2 minutes.

Drying time
20 minutes

Look through a magazine or a book of art and copy a picture you really like.

POTATO PRINTING

What you need

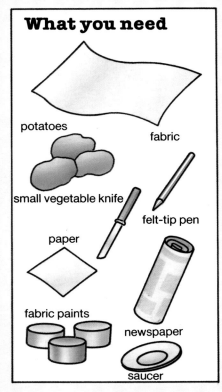

potatoes

fabric

small vegetable knife

felt-tip pen

paper

fabric paints

newspaper

saucer

3 Draw a square on the flat surface using a felt-tip pen.

6 Pour the fabric paint into the saucer.

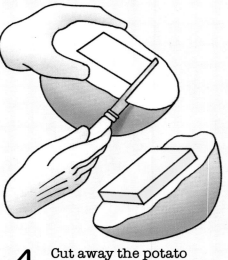

4 Cut away the potato around the outside of the line with a small vegetable knife.⊕ The remaining shape stands out above the rest of the potato. This is the part you use to print.

7 Dip the potato into the paint so that the raised surface is completely covered with color.

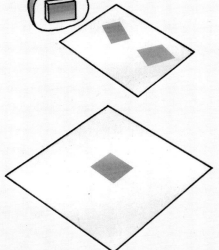

1 Wash your fabric and iron it flat.⊕

2 Wash and peel the potato. Cut it in half, making sure the surfaces are flat.

5 On a piece of newspaper, dab any surplus starch off the potato.

8 Test the print on a piece of paper. If it looks right, press firmly but gently on to the fabric.

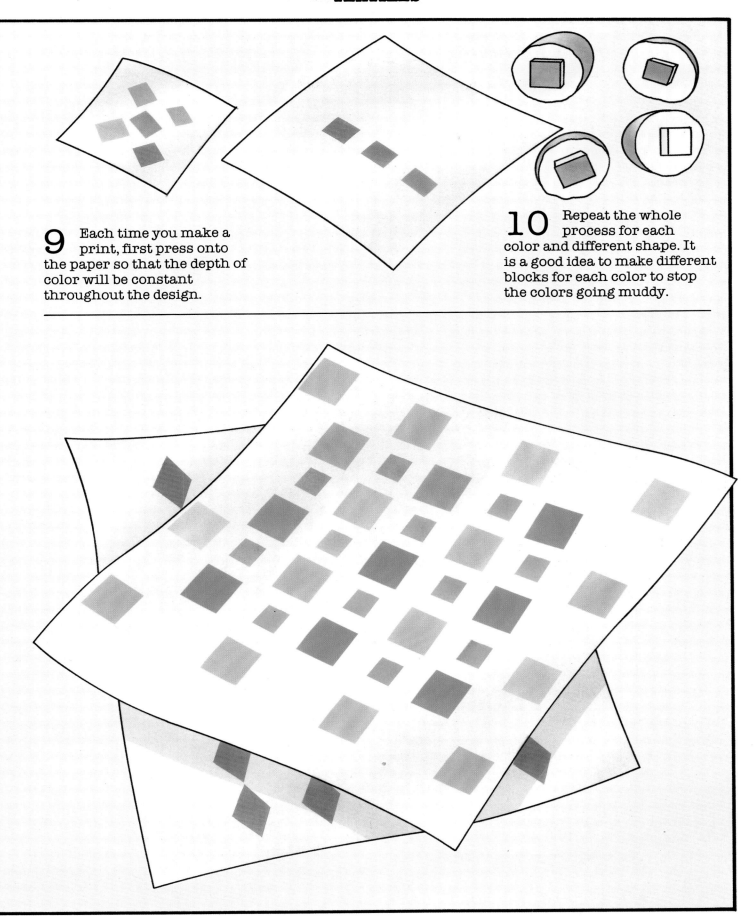

9 Each time you make a print, first press onto the paper so that the depth of color will be constant throughout the design.

10 Repeat the whole process for each color and different shape. It is a good idea to make different blocks for each color to stop the colors going muddy.

ANIMAL BOOKMARKS

These animals make unusual bookmarks and great presents.

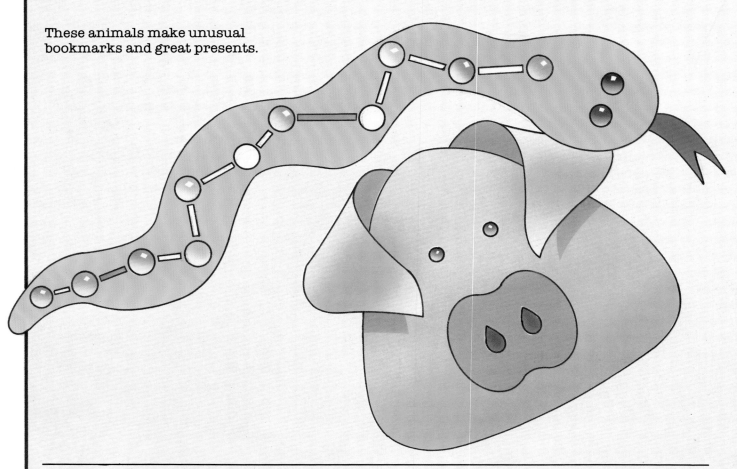

What you need

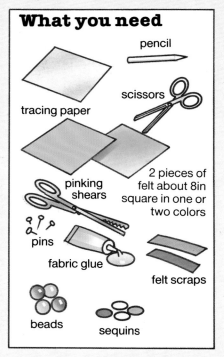

pencil

tracing paper

scissors

pinking shears

2 pieces of felt about 8in square in one or two colors

pins

fabric glue

felt scraps

beads

sequins

BOOK WORM

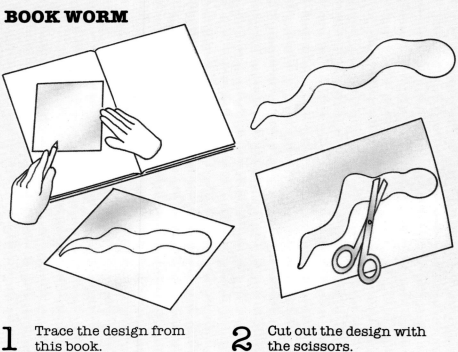

1 Trace the design from this book.

2 Cut out the design with the scissors.

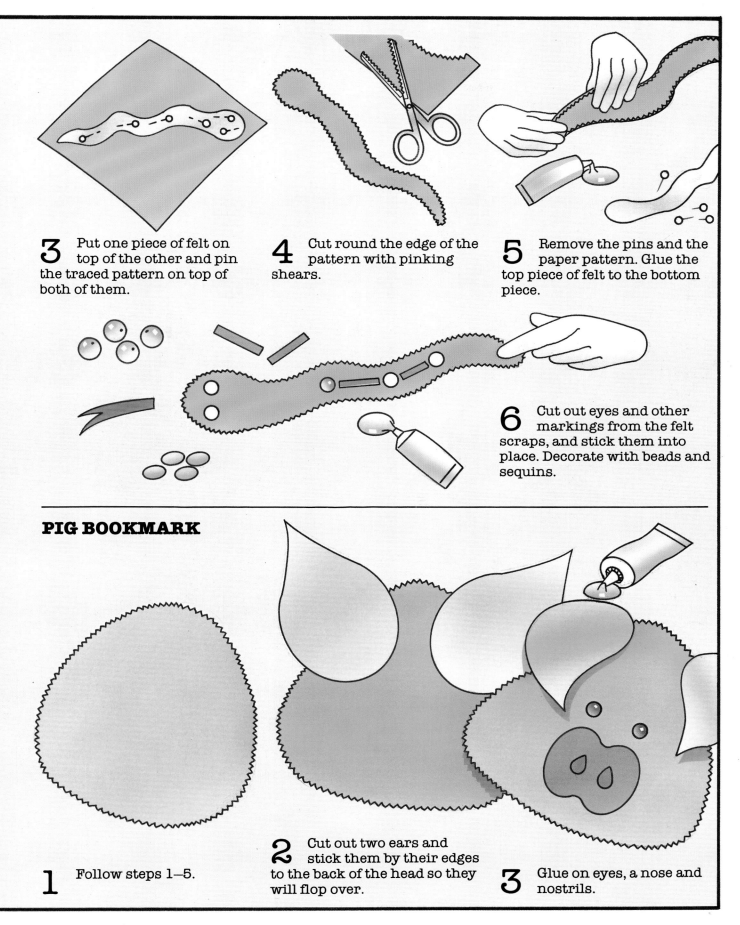

3 Put one piece of felt on top of the other and pin the traced pattern on top of both of them.

4 Cut round the edge of the pattern with pinking shears.

5 Remove the pins and the paper pattern. Glue the top piece of felt to the bottom piece.

6 Cut out eyes and other markings from the felt scraps, and stick them into place. Decorate with beads and sequins.

PIG BOOKMARK

1 Follow steps 1—5.

2 Cut out two ears and stick them by their edges to the back of the head so they will flop over.

3 Glue on eyes, a nose and nostrils.

PATCHWORK

Patchwork has been a way of using up scraps of fabric in communities for hundreds of years. To begin with, you must have pattern pieces, called templates. Follow the instructions using the square pattern and then go on to the other shapes, such as triangles, diamonds and hexagons. Information on enlarging patterns is given on p. 68.

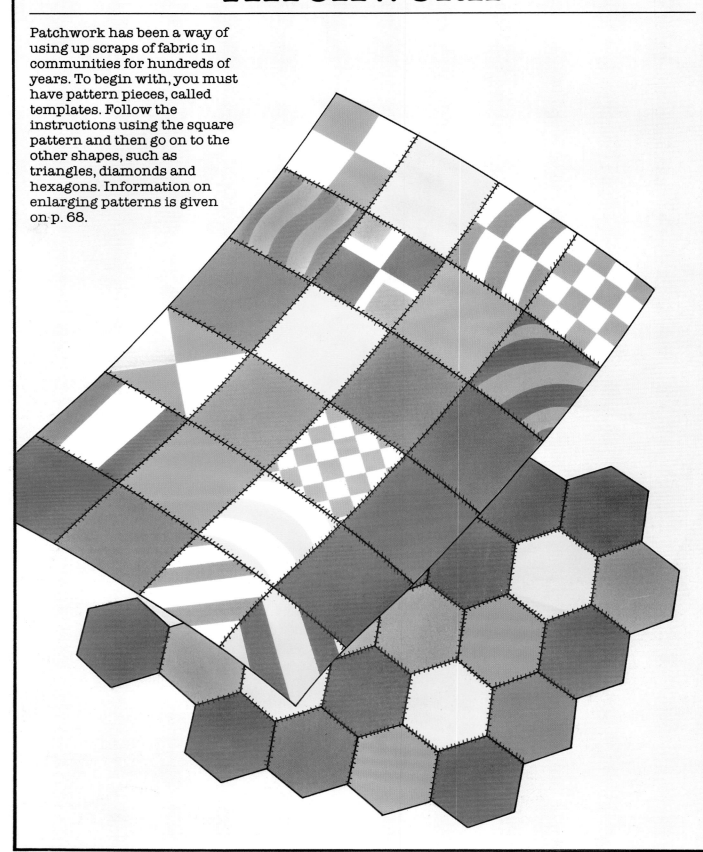

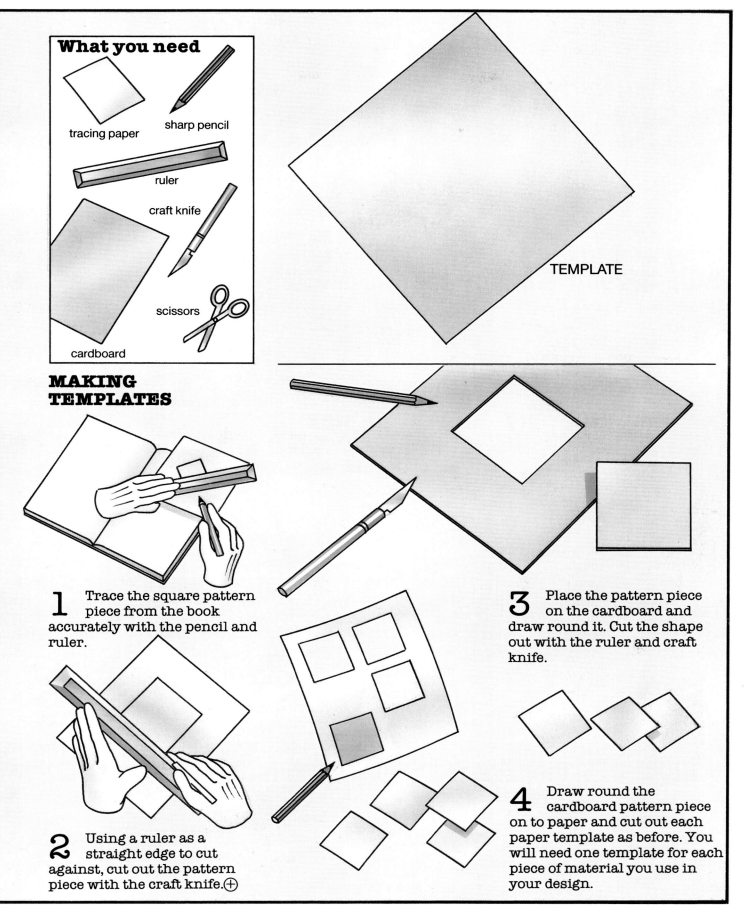

What you need

tracing paper

sharp pencil

ruler

craft knife

scissors

cardboard

TEMPLATE

MAKING TEMPLATES

1 Trace the square pattern piece from the book accurately with the pencil and ruler.

2 Using a ruler as a straight edge to cut against, cut out the pattern piece with the craft knife.⊕

3 Place the pattern piece on the cardboard and draw round it. Cut the shape out with the ruler and craft knife.

4 Draw round the cardboard pattern piece on to paper and cut out each paper template as before. You will need one template for each piece of material you use in your design.

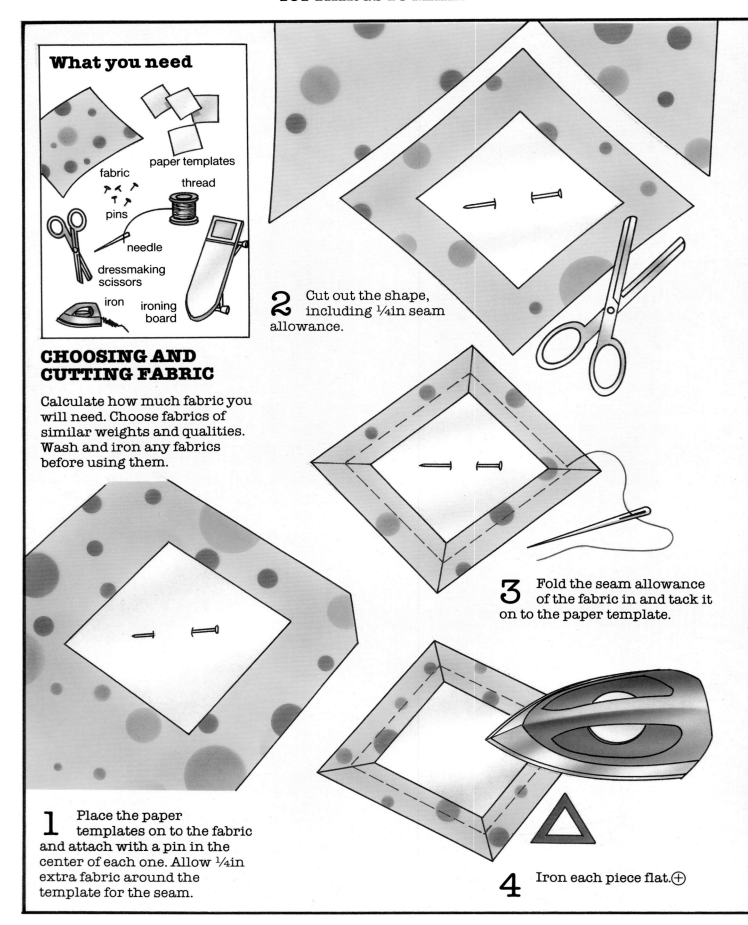

What you need

paper templates

fabric

thread

pins

needle

dressmaking scissors

iron   ironing board

CHOOSING AND CUTTING FABRIC

Calculate how much fabric you will need. Choose fabrics of similar weights and qualities. Wash and iron any fabrics before using them.

2 Cut out the shape, including ¼in seam allowance.

3 Fold the seam allowance of the fabric in and tack it on to the paper template.

1 Place the paper templates on to the fabric and attach with a pin in the center of each one. Allow ¼in extra fabric around the template for the seam.

4 Iron each piece flat.⊕

SEWING

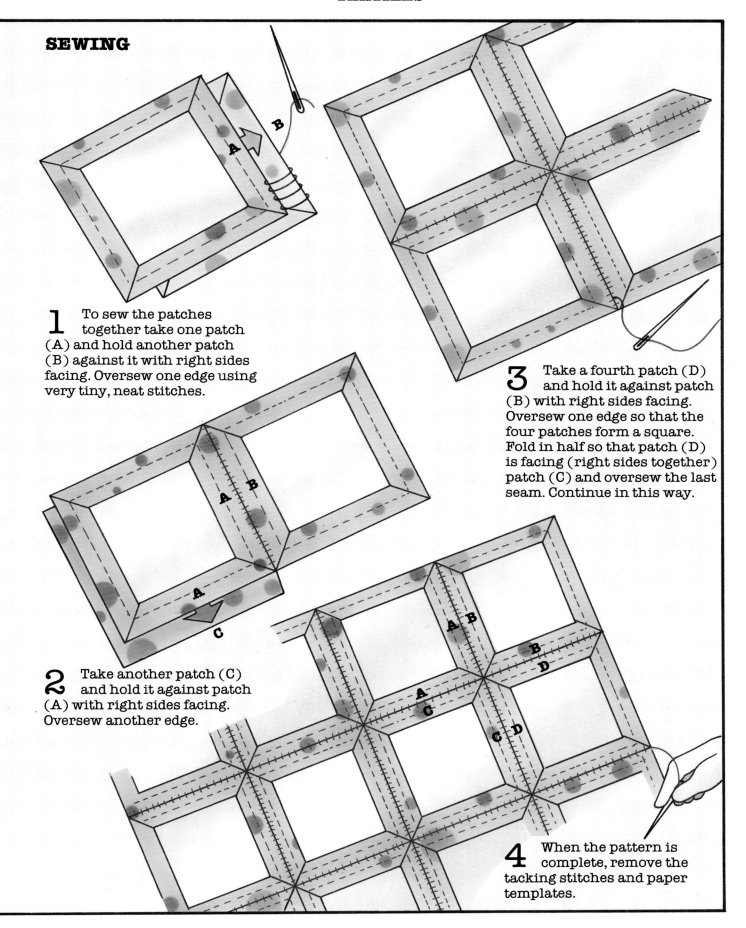

1 To sew the patches together take one patch (A) and hold another patch (B) against it with right sides facing. Oversew one edge using very tiny, neat stitches.

2 Take another patch (C) and hold it against patch (A) with right sides facing. Oversew another edge.

3 Take a fourth patch (D) and hold it against patch (B) with right sides facing. Oversew one edge so that the four patches form a square. Fold in half so that patch (D) is facing (right sides together) patch (C) and oversew the last seam. Continue in this way.

4 When the pattern is complete, remove the tacking stitches and paper templates.

APPLIQUÉ

Appliqué is used to decorate pieces of clothing, cushion covers or bedspreads. It is also used to make pictures on their own.

What you need

needle

thread

14in square of green fabric

side plate

pencil

scissors

7in square of blue fabric

pins

tracing paper

yellow fabric

DUCKS ON A DUCKPOND

1 Take the square of green fabric and sew a ¼in hem all the way around to form a square 12in × 12in.

2 Place the side plate in the center of the blue fabric and draw around it with a pencil. Cut this shape out.

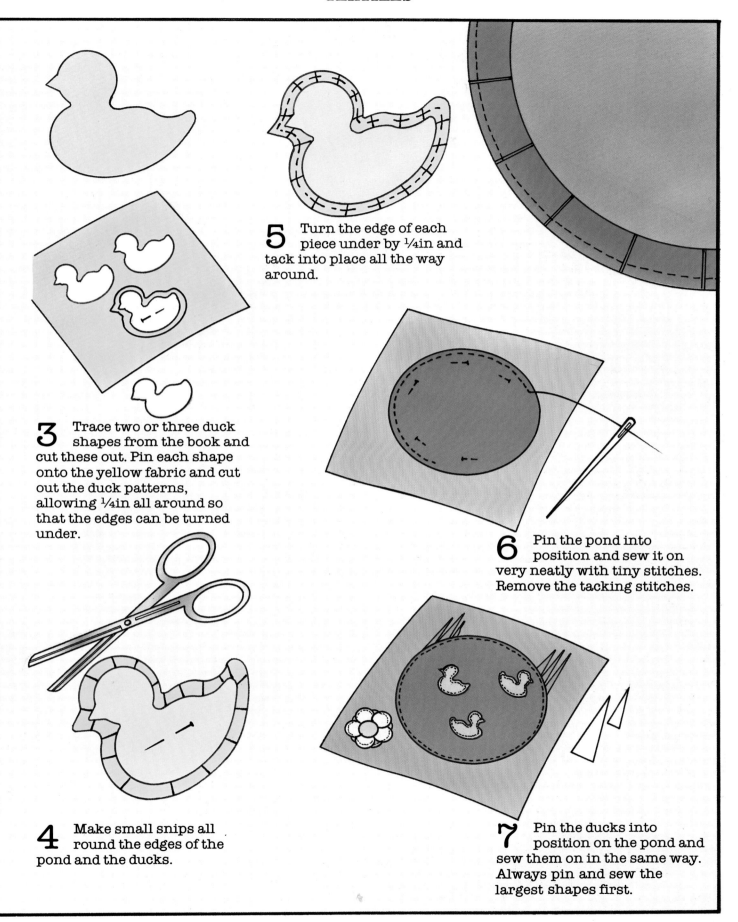

5 Turn the edge of each piece under by ¼in and tack into place all the way around.

3 Trace two or three duck shapes from the book and cut these out. Pin each shape onto the yellow fabric and cut out the duck patterns, allowing ¼in all around so that the edges can be turned under.

6 Pin the pond into position and sew it on very neatly with tiny stitches. Remove the tacking stitches.

4 Make small snips all round the edges of the pond and the ducks.

7 Pin the ducks into position on the pond and sew them on in the same way. Always pin and sew the largest shapes first.

SOCK PUPPETS

What you need

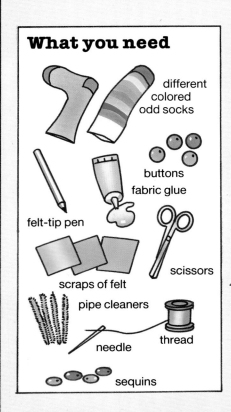

- different colored odd socks
- buttons
- fabric glue
- felt-tip pen
- scissors
- scraps of felt
- pipe cleaners
- needle
- thread
- sequins

Here is something fun to make out of all those odd socks in your drawer!

SEAL

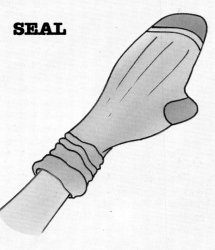

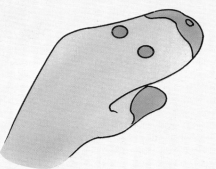

1 Put an odd grey sock on your hand, with the fingers where the toes should be and the thumb where the heel should be.

2 Bend your hand slightly and mark where the eyes and nose will be with a felt-tip pen.

3 Glue or sew on black buttons for the eyes.

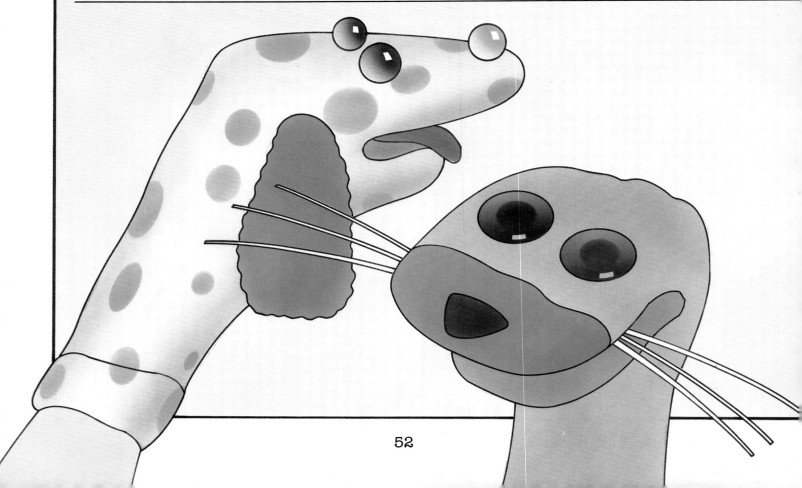

SNAKE

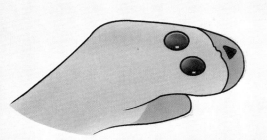

4 Cut out a felt nose and glue this into position.

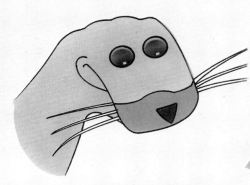

5 Thread several pipe cleaners through the end of the sock under the nose to make the whiskers.

1 Put an odd multi-colored sock on your hand as before.

2 Bend your hand slightly and mark where the eyes and the mouth will be with a felt-tip pen.

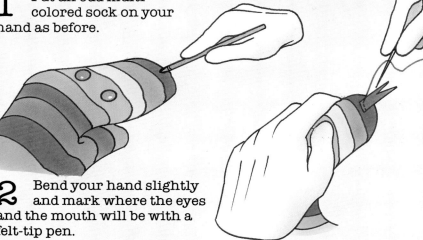

3 Cut out two slitty eyes from felt and glue them in position.

4 Cut a forked tongue from felt and sew this in position.

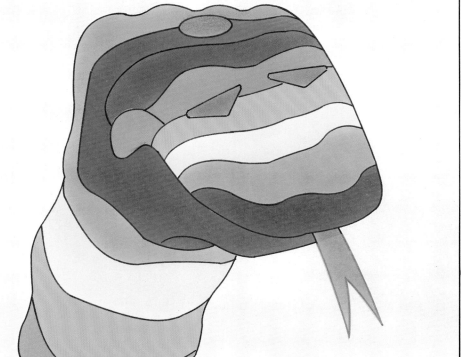

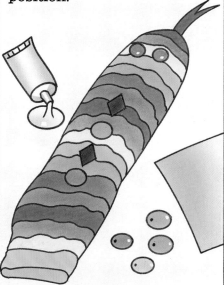

5 Decorate the body by gluing on bits of felt or sewing on different colored buttons or sequins.

TIE-DYE

Tie-dye is an ancient technique used to decorate fabric. No two tie-dye designs are ever the same. There is more information on different tie-dye techniques at the back of this section.

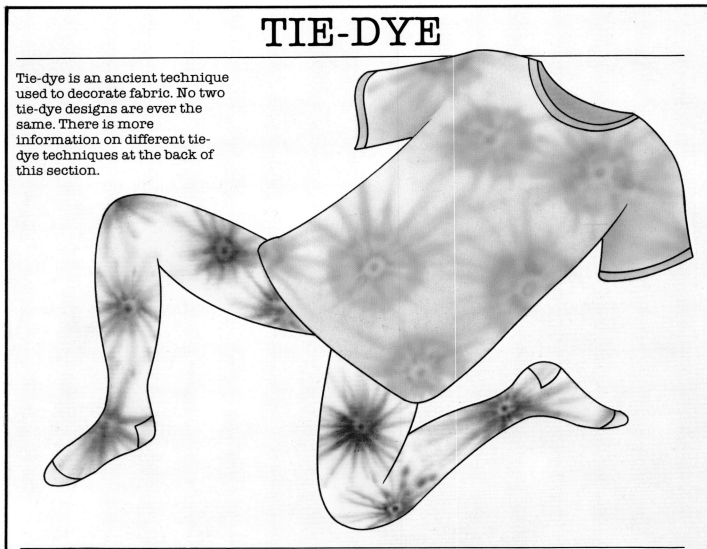

What you need

powder dye

measuring cup

water

light-coloured cotton tights

salt

cold dye fix

wooden spoon

bucket

CRAZY TIGHTS

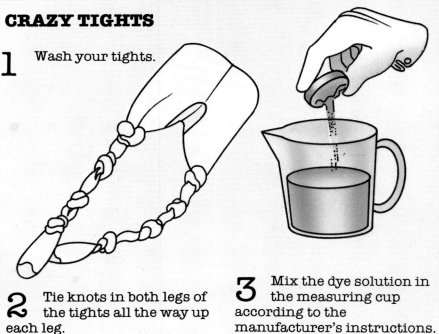

1 Wash your tights.

2 Tie knots in both legs of the tights all the way up each leg.

3 Mix the dye solution in the measuring cup according to the manufacturer's instructions.

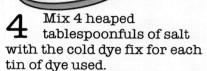

4 Mix 4 heaped tablespoonfuls of salt with the cold dye fix for each tin of dye used.

5 Pour the cold dye fix mixture into a bucket of cold water. Stir in the dye solution and mix well with a wooden spoon.

6 Add the wet tights and stir continuously for ten minutes, making sure they are fully submerged. Leave for another fifty minutes, stirring occasionally.

7 Remove the tights, rinse them and leave them to dry.

8 Untie the knots to reveal the pattern.

What you need

light-colored plain T-shirt

powder dye and cold dye fix

yarn

measuring cup

water

salt

wooden spoon

bucket

iron

ironing board

TIE-DYE T-SHIRT

1 Wash your T-shirt.

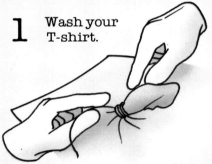

2 Draw up small clumps of fabric and tie with yarn. Remember to wind the yarn very tightly and make a secure knot.

3 Make clumps all over the front, back and sleeves of the T-shirt.

4 Mix the dye and the cold dye fix and pour into a bucket of cold water as before.

5 Repeat steps 6 and 7 as for tights.

6 Untie the yarn to reveal the pattern.

7 Iron your T-shirt. ⊕

CROSS STITCH

Cross stitch has traditionally
been used in many countries
as a way of decorating textiles.
It is also used to make
pictures.

What you need

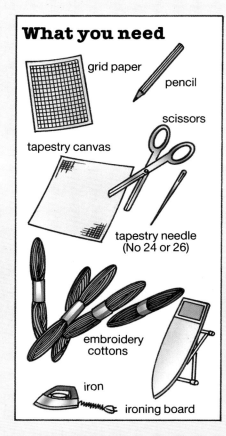

grid paper
pencil
scissors
tapestry canvas
tapestry needle (No 24 or 26)
embroidery cottons
iron
ironing board

HOME SWEET HOME

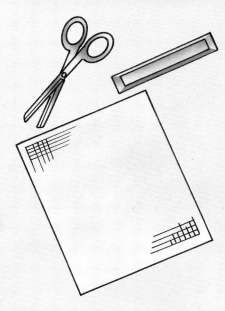

1 Cut out a piece of tapestry canvas to fit the picture pattern in the book, leaving ¼in all around so that you can hem the edges.

2 Transfer the pattern in the book on to your canvas in pencil by following the graph — count one cross as one stitch. Each cross stitch uses a square of four holes in the canvas.

3 Oversew the edges to stop them from fraying.

4 Begin your cross stitch at the top of the design and work down.

5 Thread your needle with the right color cotton and bring it through the lower right-hand side of the first stitch. Leave a short length of thread on the underside of the work and anchor it with the first few stitches.

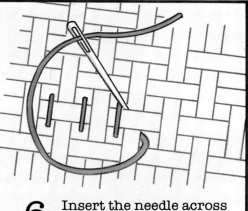

6 Insert the needle across the mesh into the next hole above and diagonally to the left.

7 Bring the needle back through the hole immediately below and take it diagonally to the right, inserting the needle through the hole immediately above the beginning of the stitch. This is your first cross stitch.

8 Continue in this way, changing colors when necessary.

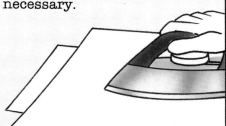

9 When the embroidery is finished, press it. Lay it face down and cover with a damp cloth. Use a warm iron on the back.⊕

SILLY, FRILLY FEET

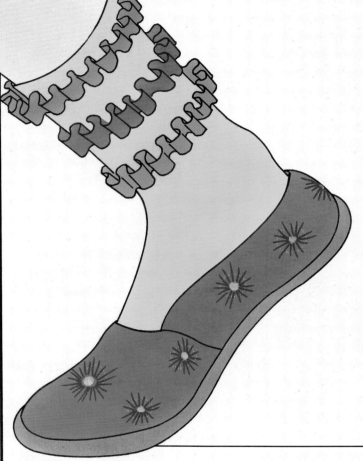

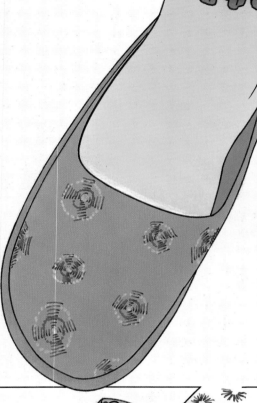

What you need

a pair of espadrilles

pencil

newspaper

fabric pens with
fine and thick tips

glitter pens
(optional)

expanding fabric
paint pens (optional)

PRINTED SHOES

Match your shoes with the
patterns on your clothes by
painting a pair of espadrilles
with a matching print.

1 Stuff the shoes with
newspaper.

2 Copy the design from
your garment on to the
shoes with a pencil.

3 Go over the design using
the different fabric paint
pens.

4 Fix the design following
the manufacturers'
instructions.

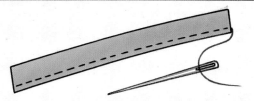

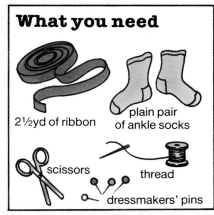

What you need

2½yd of ribbon

plain pair of ankle socks

scissors

thread

dressmakers' pins

SILLY SOCKS

Brighten up your socks with colorful ribbon frills.

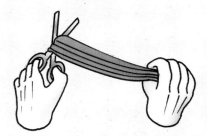

1 Cut the ribbon into six equal lengths (three for each sock).

2 Sew a line of running stitches along one edge of each piece of ribbon, as near to the edge as possible.

3 With each stitch, pull the ribbon up the thread to gather it.

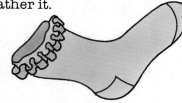

4 Starting at the back of the sock, take one ribbon and pin it all the way round, making sure the two ends overlap slightly.

5 Sew it in place with a line of back stitches, stretching the sock as you work, so it will still fit over your ankle.

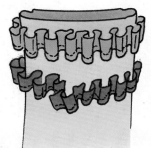

6 Neaten the ends of the ribbon. Sew the other two rows on at ¼in intervals. Repeat with the other sock.

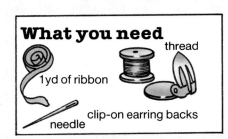

What you need

1yd of ribbon

thread

needle

clip-on earring backs

SHOE ROSETTES

1 Cut the ribbon in half.

2 Sew a line of running stitches up the center of each ribbon.

3 Gather the stitches up evenly and coil each ribbon round itself. Sew each coil together with a few running stitches.

4 Sew the ribbon coils on to the part of the clip-on earring that goes behind the ear.

5 Clip the rosettes on to your shoes.

POM-POM ANIMALS

From one pom-pom pattern you can make all sorts of animals.

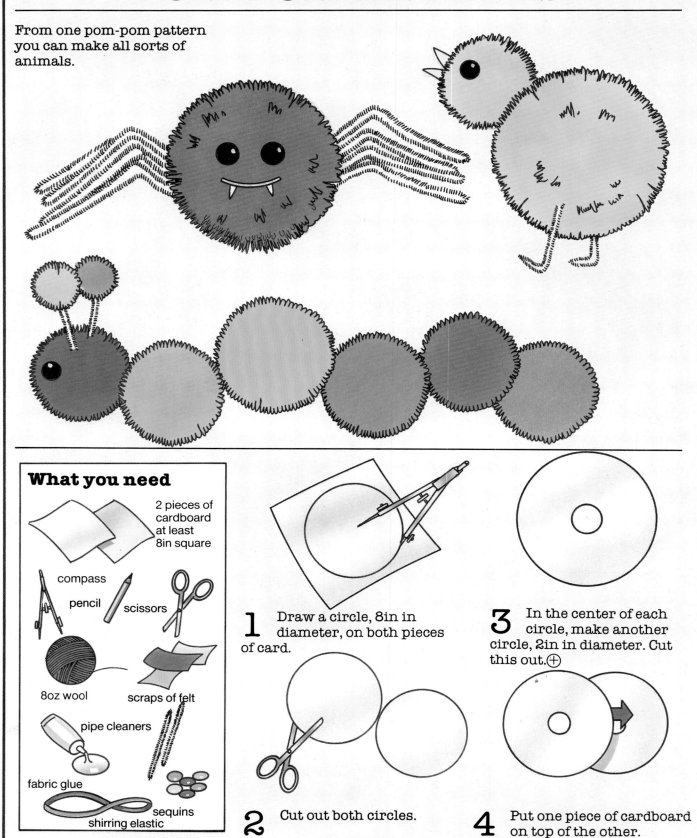

What you need

2 pieces of cardboard at least 8in square

compass

pencil

scissors

8oz wool

scraps of felt

fabric glue

pipe cleaners

sequins

shirring elastic

1 Draw a circle, 8in in diameter, on both pieces of card.

2 Cut out both circles.

3 In the center of each circle, make another circle, 2in in diameter. Cut this out. ⊕

4 Put one piece of cardboard on top of the other.

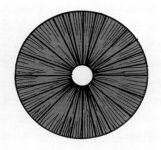

5 Tie the pieces together and wind the wool round and round through the hole in the middle until all the cardboard is thickly covered.

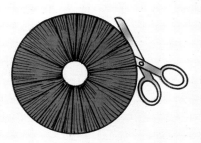

6 Carefully cut around the edge with the scissors, keeping one blade between the pieces of cardboard.

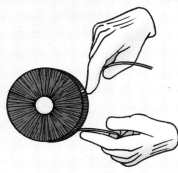

7 Pull the pieces apart slightly. Tie a piece of wool very tightly around the center of the ball.

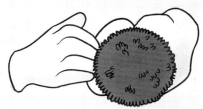

8 Remove the cardboard and fluff out the woolen ball.

EASTER CHICK

1 Make two yellow pom-poms, one slightly larger than the other.

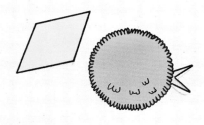

2 Cut a diamond yellow shape from felt and fold in half. Stick it in place for a beak.

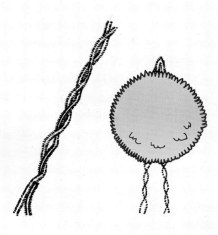

3 Make two yellow legs from pipe cleaners by twisting them around each other and through the center of the larger pom-pom to hold them in place.

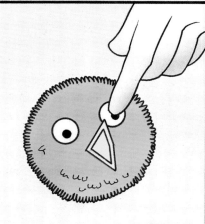

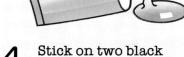

4 Stick on two black sequins for eyes.

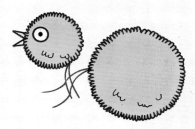

5 Firmly tie the head to the body.

6 Suspend from shirring elastic.

STUFFED TOYS

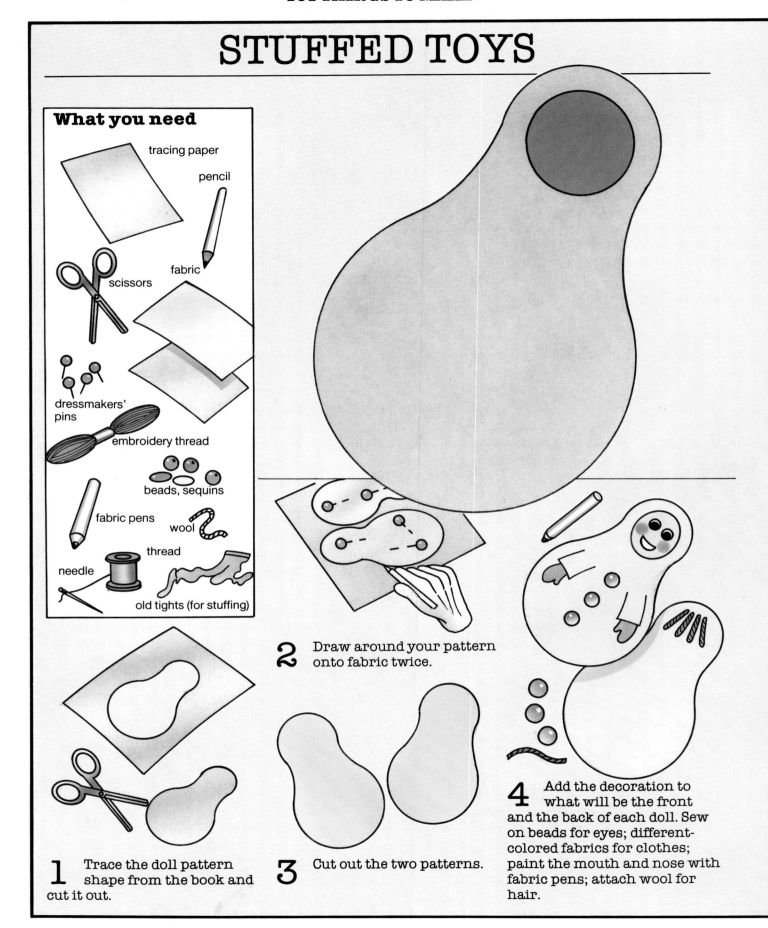

What you need

tracing paper

pencil

scissors

fabric

dressmakers' pins

embroidery thread

beads, sequins

fabric pens

wool

needle

thread

old tights (for stuffing)

1 Trace the doll pattern shape from the book and cut it out.

2 Draw around your pattern onto fabric twice.

3 Cut out the two patterns.

4 Add the decoration to what will be the front and the back of each doll. Sew on beads for eyes; different-colored fabrics for clothes; paint the mouth and nose with fabric pens; attach wool for hair.

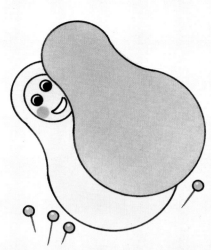

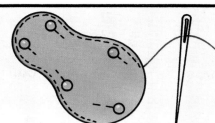

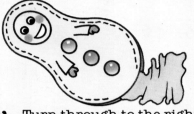

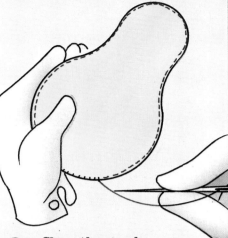

6 Sew the front to the back around three-quarters of the doll.

5 With right sides facing, position the front to the back of the doll and pin them together.

7 Turn through to the right side and fill with stuffing.

8 Close the gap by oversewing very neatly.

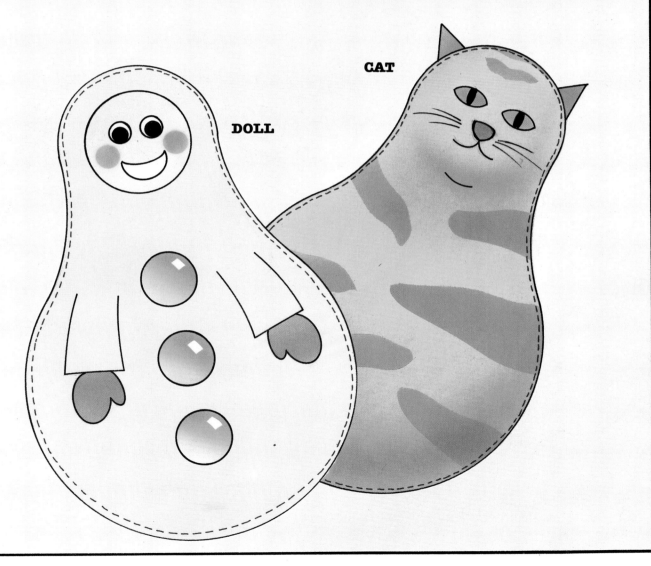

DOLL

CAT

TOAD BAG

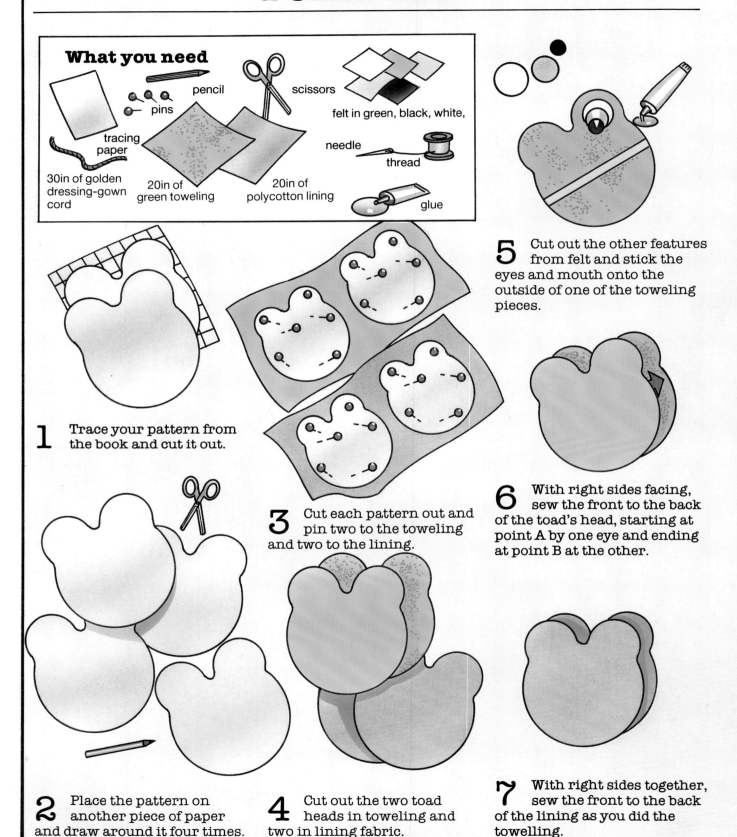

What you need

pencil

pins

tracing paper

scissors

felt in green, black, white,

needle

thread

30in of golden dressing-gown cord

20in of green toweling

20in of polycotton lining

glue

1 Trace your pattern from the book and cut it out.

2 Place the pattern on another piece of paper and draw around it four times.

3 Cut each pattern out and pin two to the toweling and two to the lining.

4 Cut out the two toad heads in toweling and two in lining fabric.

5 Cut out the other features from felt and stick the eyes and mouth onto the outside of one of the toweling pieces.

6 With right sides facing, sew the front to the back of the toad's head, starting at point A by one eye and ending at point B at the other.

7 With right sides together, sew the front to the back of the lining as you did the towelling.

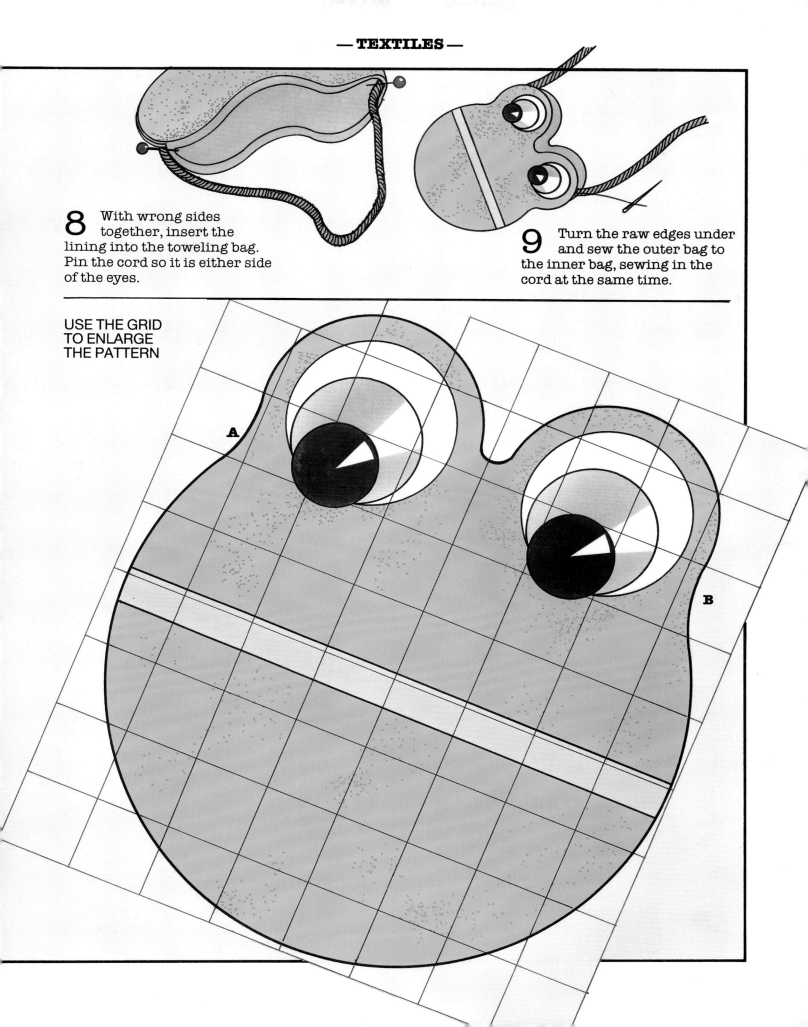

8 With wrong sides together, insert the lining into the toweling bag. Pin the cord so it is either side of the eyes.

9 Turn the raw edges under and sew the outer bag to the inner bag, sewing in the cord at the same time.

USE THE GRID TO ENLARGE THE PATTERN

A

B

MORE IDEAS

T-SHIRTS (pages 40—41)

There are many different kinds of fabric paints you can use to decorate your clothes. Most fabric paints are only suitable for light-colored fabrics as they absorb the background material color.

Expanding paint sits on the surface of the fabric and when heated it rises above the surface and has a slightly rubbery texture. Because it doesn't sink into the fabric, expanding paint is very effective on dark-colored materials.

Glitter paint comes in a tube with a long nozzle. You paint it on as if using a brush. It is a glue-like substance in which particles of glitter are suspended. This is an ideal paint for theatrical costumes.

Iron-on transfer paints are applied to paper. When you have painted your design, turn the paper over and iron the design on to your fabric.

PRINTING ON FABRIC (pages 42—43)

Blocks or stamps for printing can be made from almost anything, including wood, lino, rubber, cork and fruit and vegetables.

You can make printing blocks from onions, pears, apples or peppers cut in half. The shape of the fruit or vegetable becomes your design.

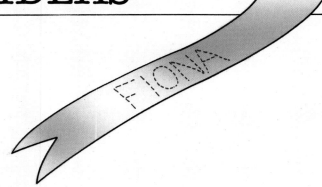

BOOKMARKS (pages 44—45)

Make other bookmarks by cutting a piece of wide ribbon and sewing a name on to it.

PATCHWORK (pages 46—49)

Go to local museums to look at interesting examples of patchwork.

When making patchwork, begin with small items, like a doll's beadspread or bag, and then go on to bigger projects. You could even make a spread for your own bed.

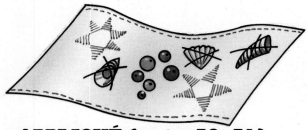

APPLIQUÉ (pages 50—51)

Your appliqué design can be embellished with decorative embroidery stitches, trimmings, beads, shells, sequins and mirrors.

SOCK PUPPETS (pages 52—53)

You can also turn mittens into puppets or decorate the fingers of gloves to look like people or finger puppets.

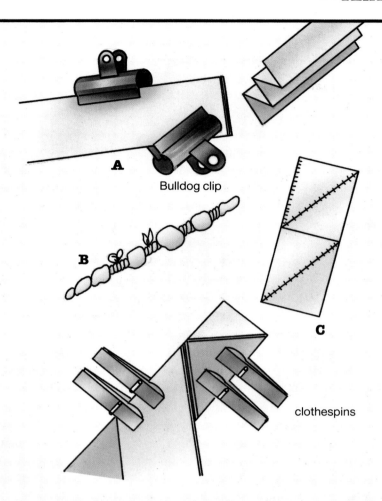

Bulldog clip

clothespins

SILLY, FRILLY FEET (pages 58—59)

There are lots of ways in which you can decorate your footwear:

A Thread ribbon or sew beads onto fabric shoes.
B Embroider your name in bright wool onto a dull pair of socks.
C Make and sew pom-poms on the back of ankle socks.
D Paint glitter paint onto fabric or plastic shoes.

POM-POMS (pages 60—61)

There are lots of other animals you could make with pom-poms, such as a robin, a caterpillar or a snake.

Join different-colored pom-poms together to make a snake. Cut out a red felt forked tongue and attach.

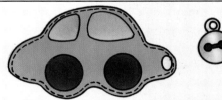

STUFFED TOYS (pages 62—63)

As well as dolls, you could make animals, teddy bears or cars. Place a bell inside the toy while you are stuffing it, to make it jingle.

TIE-DYE (pages 54—55)

Here are some different ways to tie-dye fabric:

A Fold the fabric in a concertina pattern and hold in place with bulldog clips.
B Roll your fabric into a sausage shape and tie yarn around it at intervals.
C Fold the fabric in different ways and then overstitch along the folded edges.
D Crumple the fabric into a ball and bind it tightly. Dye it once and then bind it again to dip into a second color.

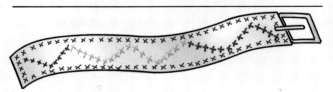

CROSS STITCH (pages 56—57)

You can use cross stitch to make all sorts of pictures or to decorate an article of clothing.

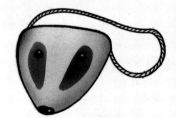

TOAD BAG (pages 64—65)

You could design your own bag, using a favorite character from a book or a film.

SPECIAL TECHNIQUE

ENLARGING PATTERNS

Most patterns you find in books will need to be enlarged before you can use them. You will need some dressmakers' grid paper and a pencil.

First mark with dots the points where pattern lines and the smaller grid lines meet onto the larger grid paper.

When you are sure that everything is marked in correctly, join the dots up into lines, making sure you are following each square from the book exactly.

Remember to put in seam allowances and other extra pattern markings.

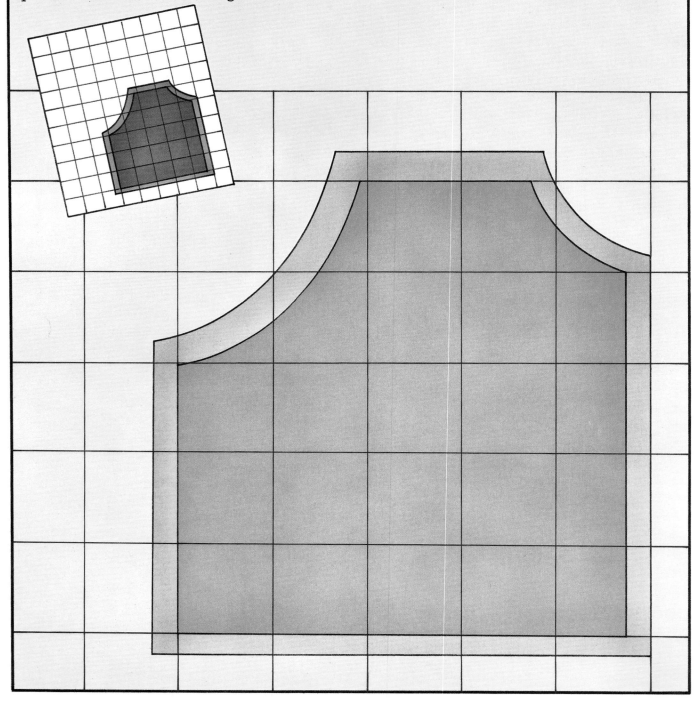

3
Paper, Print and Paint

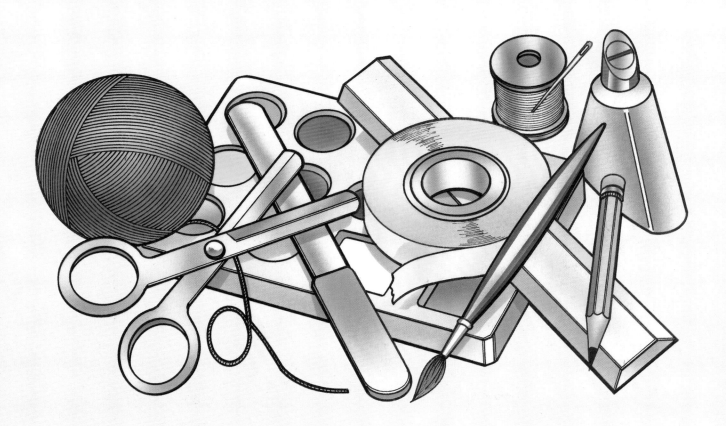

INTRODUCTION

The purpose of this section is to introduce you to the fun and delight of using paper, print and paint in many different ways. Some of the ideas are very simple and require the minimum equipment, other ideas are more complex and need greater investment in both time and money.

The crafts involved include decorating paper with texture, block and stencil printing, and learning how to make bowls, badges and pop-up cards.

This section is intended to be used as a starting point to inspire as well as instruct you and lead you on to create your own wonderful designs.

Before you start:

* Read all the instructions carefully.
* Collect all your tools and materials together. Remember, if you are using oil-based paints you will need paint thinner to dilute paints and wash brushes.
* Wear an apron or overall.
* Cover your work surface with newspaper and have a place where you can dry wet paintings.
* Clean up after yourself.
* Look out for this sign ⊕ throughout the instructions. It means "be careful"!

MATERIALS AND TOOLS

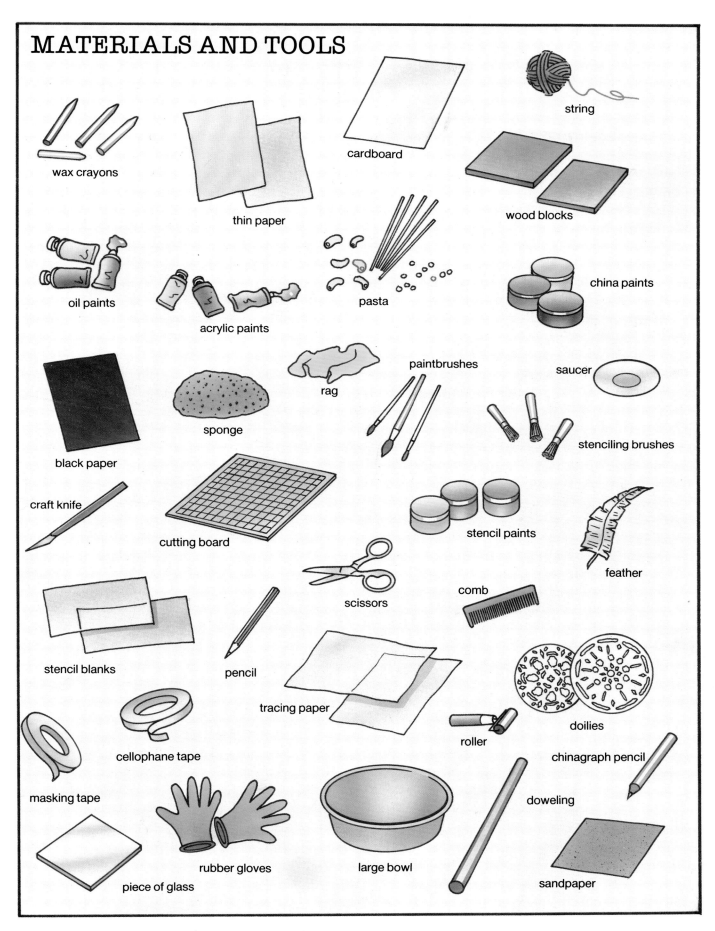

string

wax crayons

thin paper

cardboard

wood blocks

oil paints

acrylic paints

pasta

china paints

black paper

sponge

rag

paintbrushes

saucer

stenciling brushes

craft knife

cutting board

stencil paints

feather

scissors

comb

stencil blanks

pencil

tracing paper

roller

doilies

chinagraph pencil

masking tape

cellophane tape

rubber gloves

large bowl

doweling

piece of glass

sandpaper

DECORATING PAPER WITH TEXTURES

You can create beautiful patterns and interesting textures on paper with paint and a variety of everyday objects.

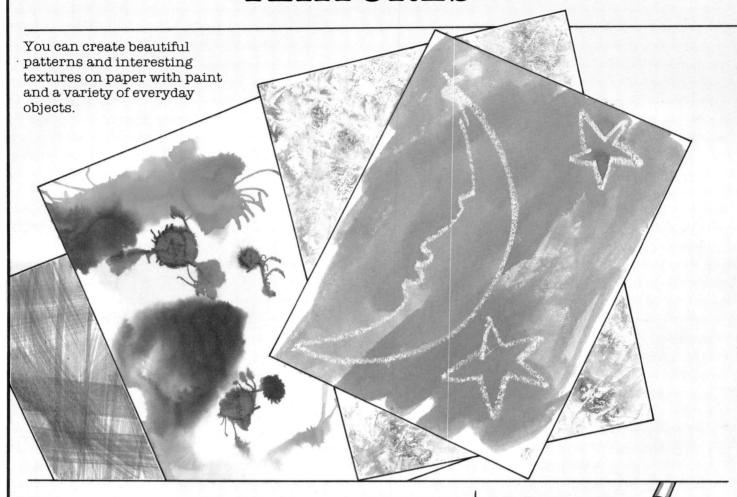

What you need

wax crayons

paper

watercolor paints

saucer

string

paintbrushes

old comb

cork

piece of knitted fabric

old toothbrush

sponge

feather

RESIST PATTERN

1 Draw a pattern on the paper with a wax crayon.

2 Dilute a colored paint in the saucer and paint a wash of color over the wax crayon. The wax pattern will show through.

BLOB PATTERN

1 Wet your paper all over.

2 Load a paintbrush with paint and let drops fall on the wet paper. As the paint hits the paper it will spread into a blob.

STRING PATTERN

1 Fill a saucer with paint and dip the string in the saucer so it is covered in paint.

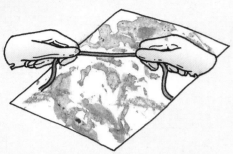

2 Hold the string tightly over the paper and then let go so a pattern splats onto the paper.

CORK PATTERN

1 Cover the paper with paint, using a large brush.

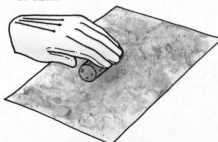

2 When the paint is nearly dry, take a cork and roll it over the paper. It will leave a mottled pattern.

SPONGE PATTERN

1 Cover the paper with paint, using a large brush.

2 Take a dry sponge and dab it in the paint. As you do so color will lift off, leaving a speckled pattern.

FLICKING

1 Dip your paintbrush in a saucerful of colored paint and flick it onto a sheet of paper.

2 Use brushes of different thicknesses and change colors to add interest.

COMBING

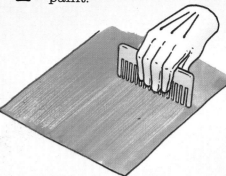

1 Cover the paper with paint.

2 Take an old comb and drag it through the wet paint. Be careful not to press too hard or you will rip the paper.

3 An old toothbrush can be used in the same way.

KNITTED FABRIC

1 Pour your paint into a saucer.

2 Dip the piece of knitted fabric in the paint and dab it on the paper.

3 A feather can be used in the same way.

STENCILING

FABRIC FRIEZE

What you need

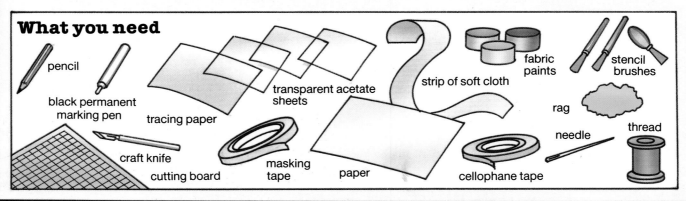

pencil

black permanent
marking pen

tracing paper

transparent acetate
sheets

strip of soft cloth

fabric
paints

stencil
brushes

rag

craft knife

cutting board

masking
tape

paper

cellophane tape

needle

thread

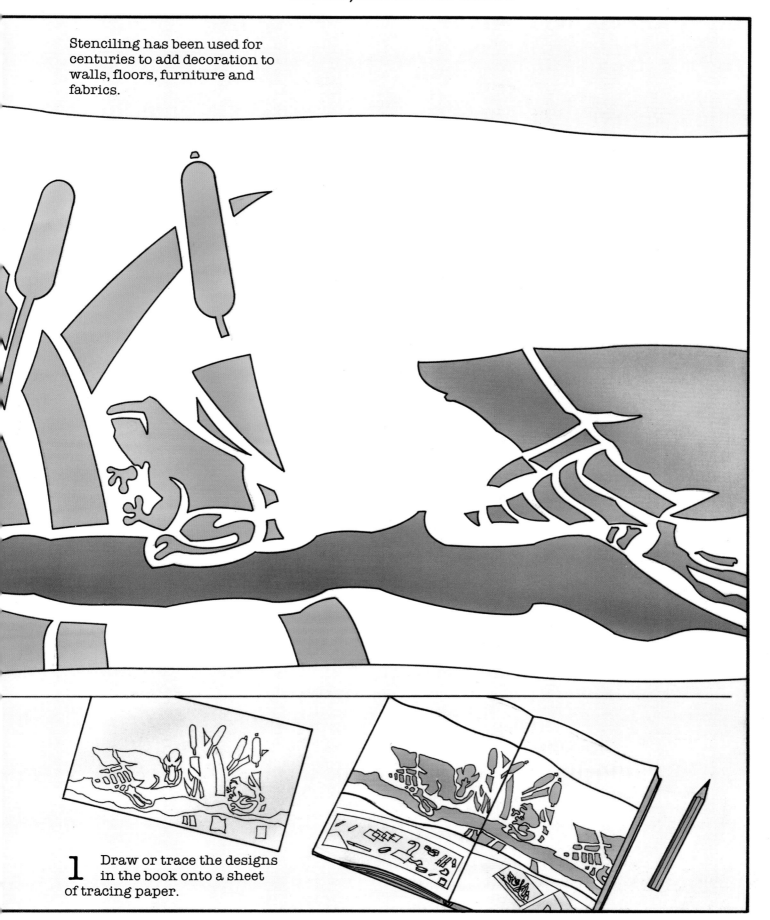

Stenciling has been used for centuries to add decoration to walls, floors, furniture and fabrics.

1 Draw or trace the designs in the book onto a sheet of tracing paper.

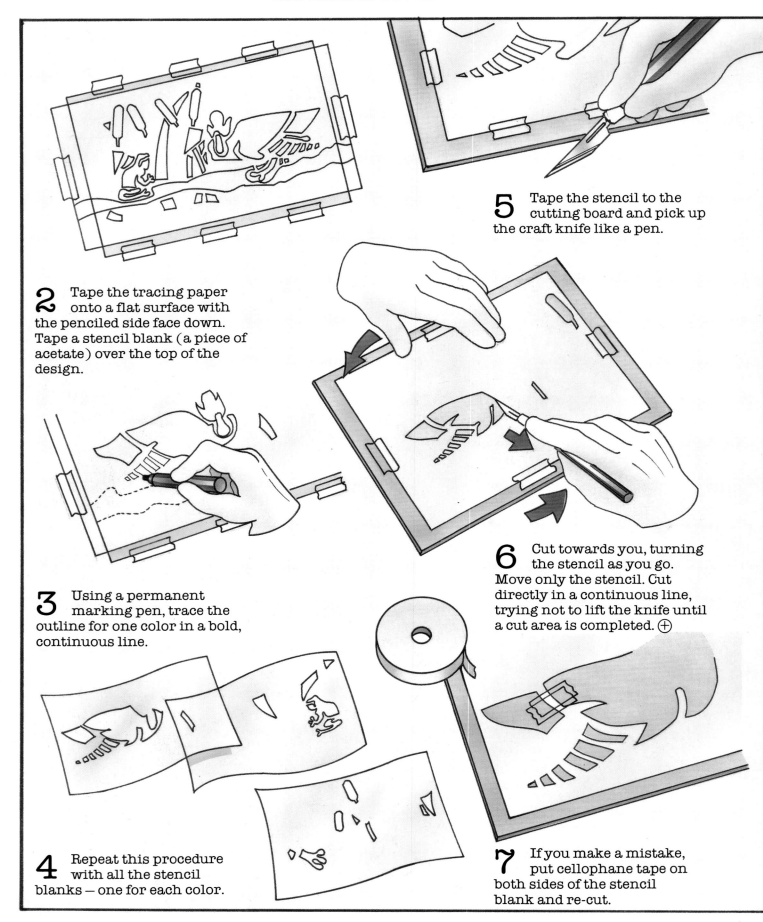

5 Tape the stencil to the cutting board and pick up the craft knife like a pen.

2 Tape the tracing paper onto a flat surface with the penciled side face down. Tape a stencil blank (a piece of acetate) over the top of the design.

3 Using a permanent marking pen, trace the outline for one color in a bold, continuous line.

4 Repeat this procedure with all the stencil blanks — one for each color.

6 Cut towards you, turning the stencil as you go. Move only the stencil. Cut directly in a continuous line, trying not to lift the knife until a cut area is completed. ⊕

7 If you make a mistake, put cellophane tape on both sides of the stencil blank and re-cut.

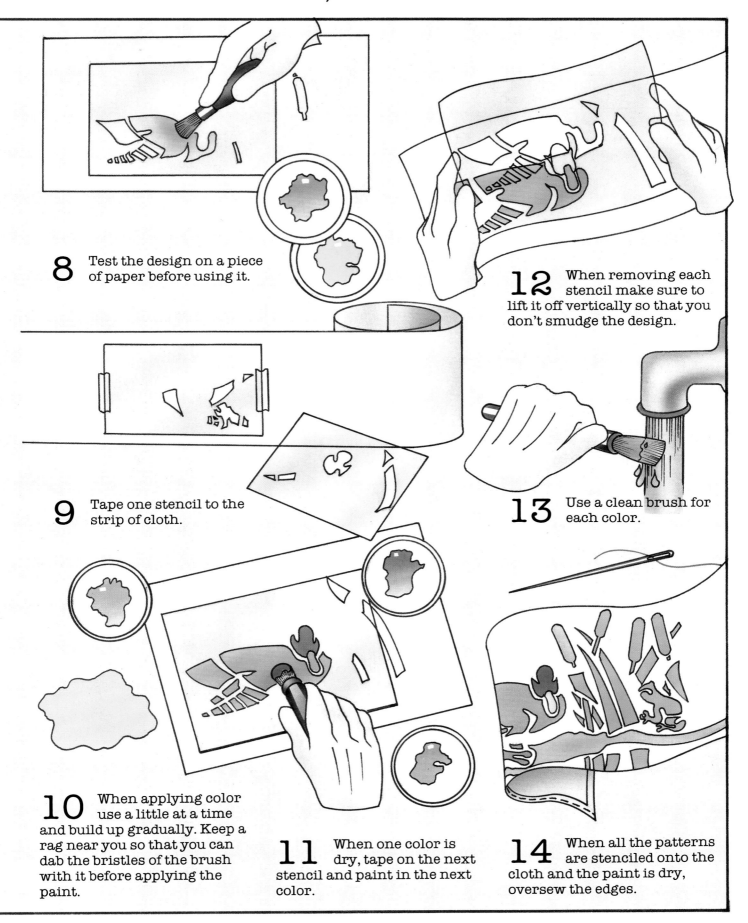

8 Test the design on a piece of paper before using it.

9 Tape one stencil to the strip of cloth.

10 When applying color use a little at a time and build up gradually. Keep a rag near you so that you can dab the bristles of the brush with it before applying the paint.

11 When one color is dry, tape on the next stencil and paint in the next color.

12 When removing each stencil make sure to lift it off vertically so that you don't smudge the design.

13 Use a clean brush for each color.

14 When all the patterns are stenciled onto the cloth and the paint is dry, oversew the edges.

BROOCHES AND BADGES

What you need

pencil

white cardboard

scissors

glue

clear nail polish

safety pin

cellophane tape

felt-tip pens

CARD BROOCHES

1 Draw your brooch design onto the cardboard with a pencil.

2 Cut out the design. Draw around the brooch onto a second piece of cardboard and cut out.

3 Stick the two pieces of cardboard together. Color in the design with felt-tip pens.

4 Varnish the front of the brooch with clear nail polish.

5 Tape the safety pin to the back of the brooch.

What you need

scissors

glue stick

your favorite comic

clear nail polish

black cardboard

safety pin   cellophane tape

COMIC BADGES

1 Cut out the character from your comic that you would like to make into a badge.

2 Stick the picture onto black cardboard and cut around it.

3 Cover the front and back with clear nail polish.

4 Tape a safety pin onto the back.

HI!

RUBBINGS

Brass, bronze and stone carvings can be found on old churches and other buildings. By placing paper over these carvings and rubbing with a wax crayon you can take away paper images of them. Before you begin you must ask permission from the caretaker or owner of the building.

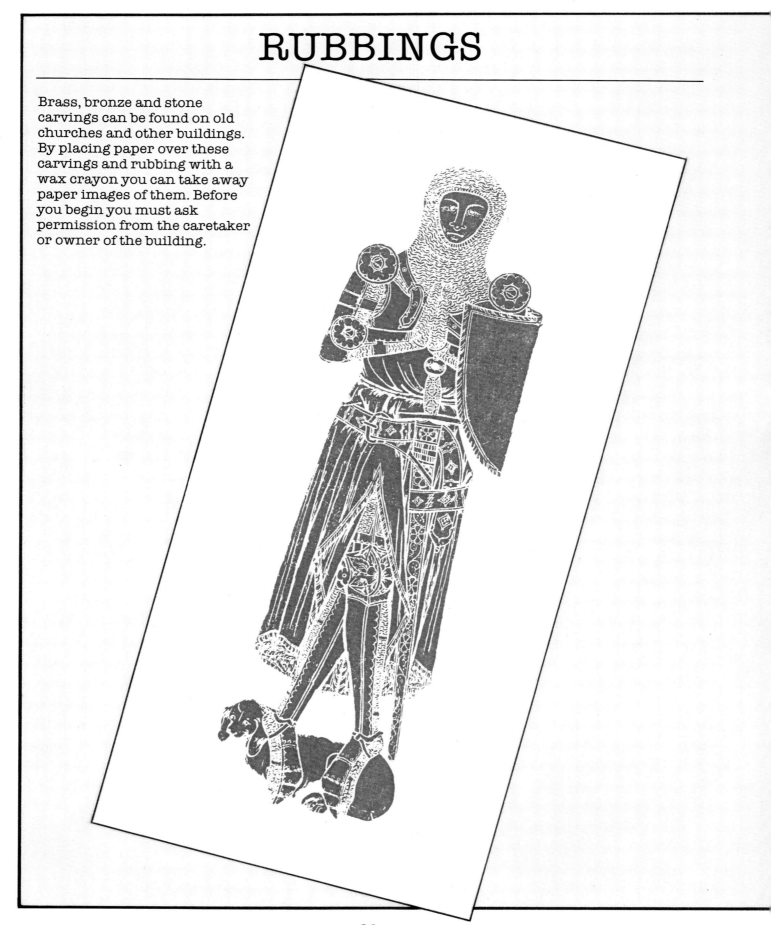

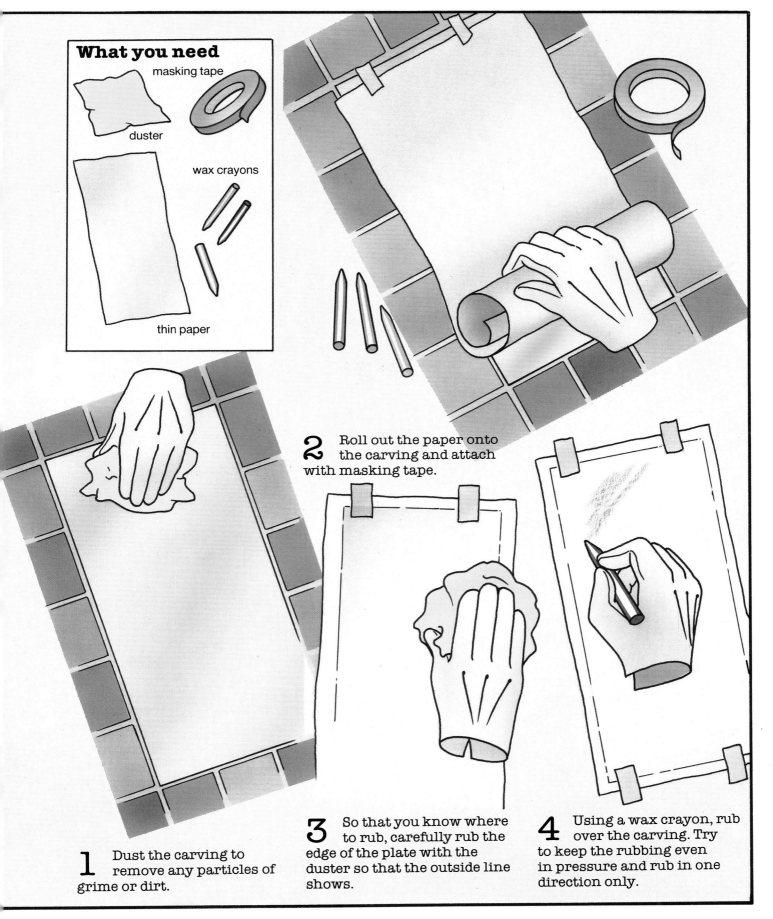

What you need

masking tape

duster

wax crayons

thin paper

2 Roll out the paper onto the carving and attach with masking tape.

1 Dust the carving to remove any particles of grime or dirt.

3 So that you know where to rub, carefully rub the edge of the plate with the duster so that the outside line shows.

4 Using a wax crayon, rub over the carving. Try to keep the rubbing even in pressure and rub in one direction only.

MARBLING PAPER

What you need

saucers

lots of newspaper

artists' oil paints

paint thinner

paintbrush

a large bowl of water

rubber gloves

plain white paper

1 Cover your work surface with lots of newspaper. Marbling is fun but very messy! You need somewhere to put all the finished work while it is drying.

2 Squeeze out a little color onto the saucer and dilute with a little thinner.

3 Drop the color onto the surface of the water with a paintbrush — it will float.

4 Mix a second color and add it to the water, stirring it gently with the end of the paintbrush.

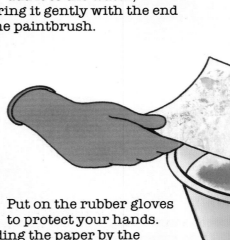

5 Put on the rubber gloves to protect your hands. Holding the paper by the corners, put it on the surface of the water. The paint will stick to the paper.

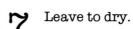

6 Lift the paper off quickly, making sure it remains vertical so that the pattern doesn't run.

7 Leave to dry.

8 Add more colors to the water and repeat steps 5–7.

9 Clean all brushes and utensils with thinner.

MAKING AND USING BLOCKS

By attaching various objects to a flat piece of wood and covering them with an even layer of paint, you can print all sorts of exciting patterns and designs.

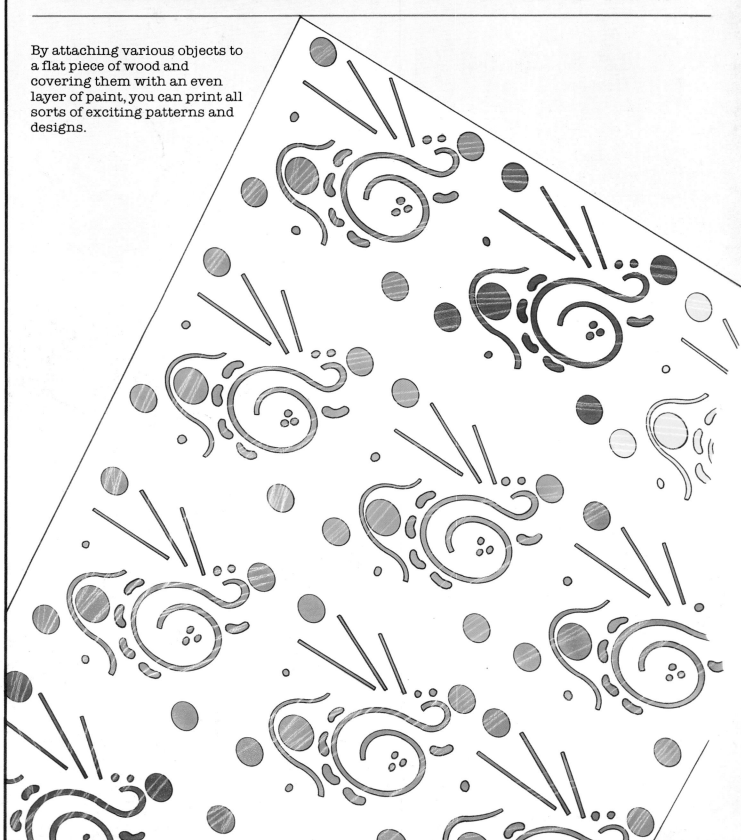

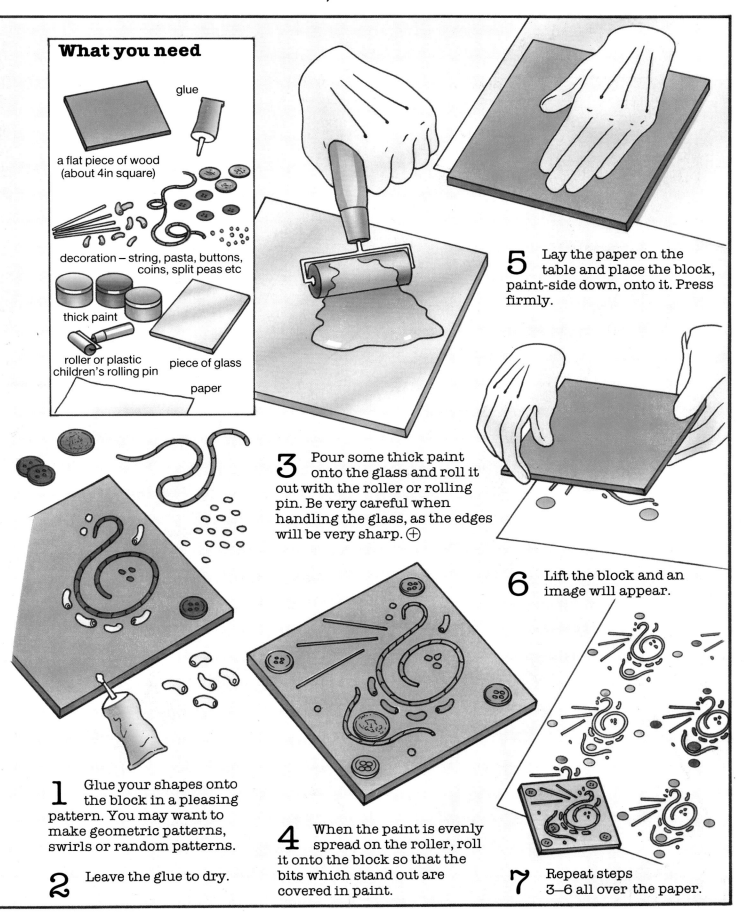

What you need

glue

a flat piece of wood (about 4in square)

decoration – string, pasta, buttons, coins, split peas etc

thick paint

roller or plastic children's rolling pin

piece of glass

paper

3 Pour some thick paint onto the glass and roll it out with the roller or rolling pin. Be very careful when handling the glass, as the edges will be very sharp. ⊕

5 Lay the paper on the table and place the block, paint-side down, onto it. Press firmly.

6 Lift the block and an image will appear.

1 Glue your shapes onto the block in a pleasing pattern. You may want to make geometric patterns, swirls or random patterns.

2 Leave the glue to dry.

4 When the paint is evenly spread on the roller, roll it onto the block so that the bits which stand out are covered in paint.

7 Repeat steps 3–6 all over the paper.

PAINTED CHINA

What you need

chinagraph pencil

paintbrushes

newspaper

clear artists' varnish

plain china plates or mugs

ceramic paints

thinner

Painting your own china is easy and the results can be stunning. Before you start, see page 99 for more information on working with ceramic paints.

1 Lay out plenty of newspaper on a large work surface.

2 Using the chinagraph pencil, draw your design onto the china.

3 Paint in the larger areas of color. Ceramic paints look better slightly dappled, as it is very hard to get a flat, even surface over a large area.

4 Once the large area has been painted, add the detail. Do not overload the brush with paint, but gradually build up color.

5 Add a fine black outline if needed for fine markings and patterns.

6 Leave to dry.

7 Wash paintbrushes in thinner.

8 Varnish with clear artists' varnish to give extra protection.

POP-UP CARDS

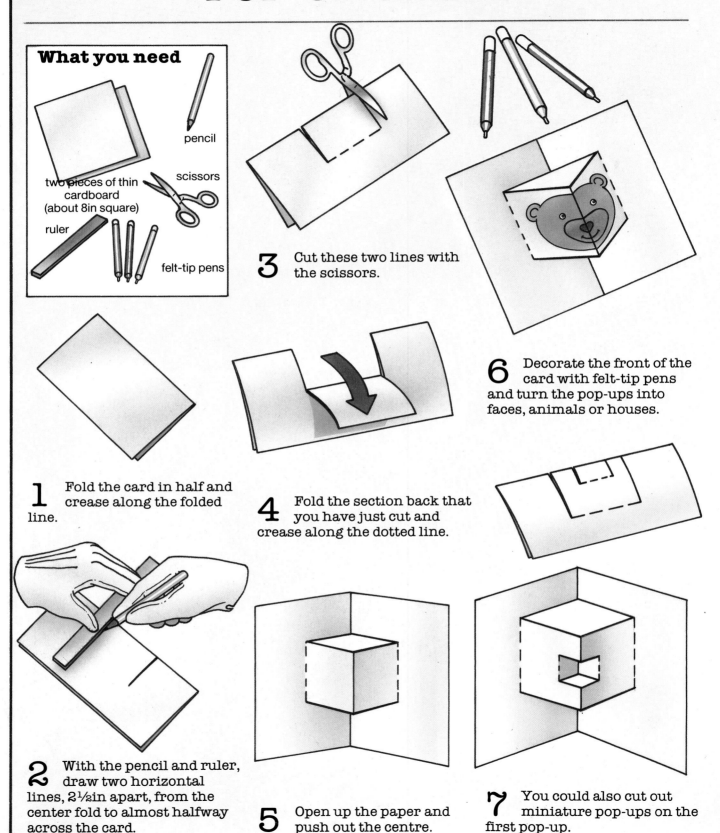

What you need

two pieces of thin cardboard (about 8in square)

pencil

scissors

ruler

felt-tip pens

3 Cut these two lines with the scissors.

6 Decorate the front of the card with felt-tip pens and turn the pop-ups into faces, animals or houses.

1 Fold the card in half and crease along the folded line.

4 Fold the section back that you have just cut and crease along the dotted line.

2 With the pencil and ruler, draw two horizontal lines, 2½in apart, from the center fold to almost halfway across the card.

5 Open up the paper and push out the centre.

7 You could also cut out miniature pop-ups on the first pop-up.

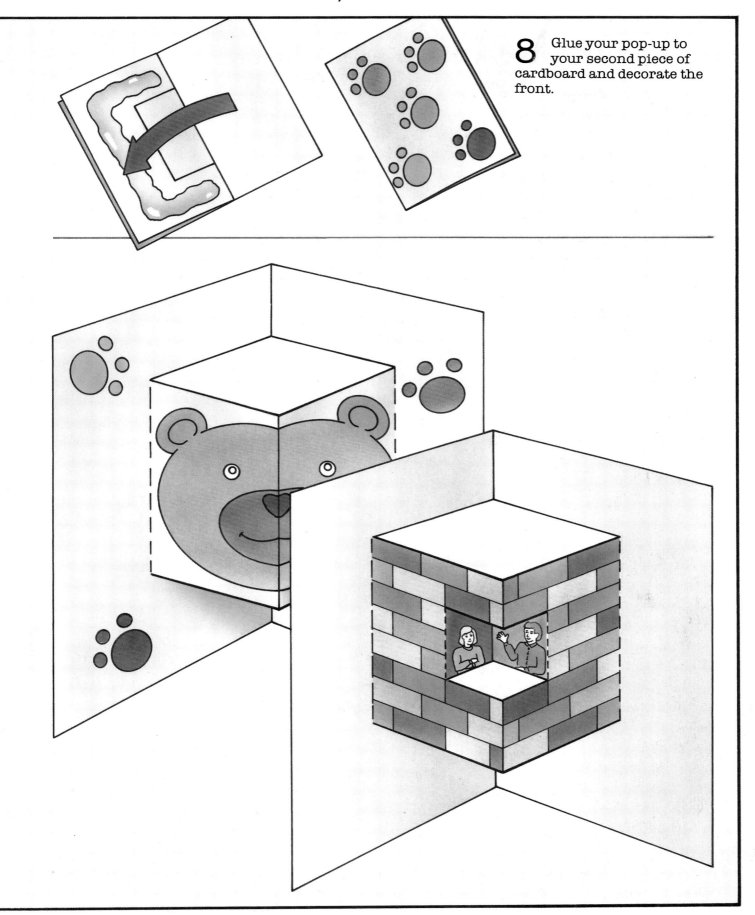

8 Glue your pop-up to your second piece of cardboard and decorate the front.

ANGEL MOBILE

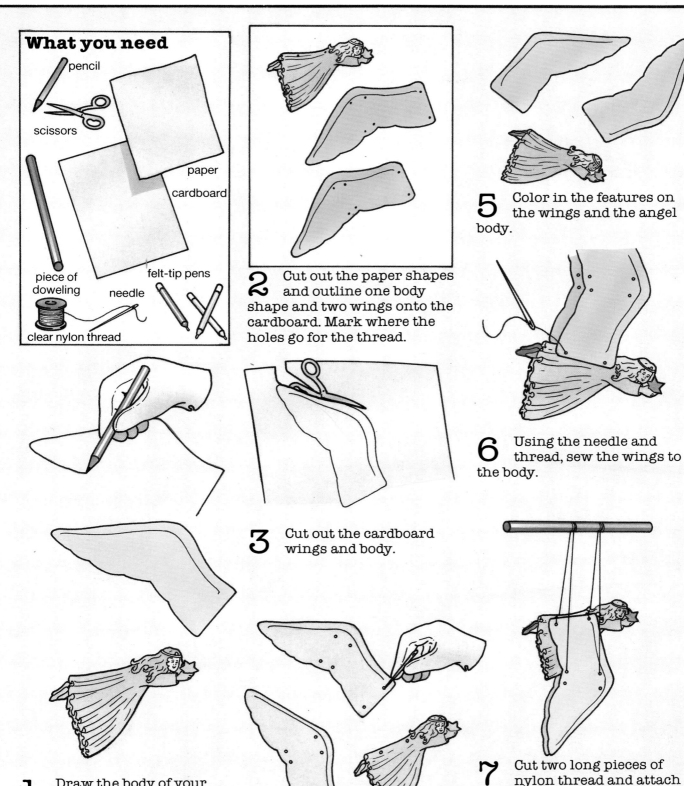

What you need

pencil

scissors

paper

cardboard

piece of doweling

felt-tip pens

needle

clear nylon thread

1 Draw the body of your angel onto paper. Use the picture in the book as a guideline. Draw the wings separately, making them about a third larger in size than the body of the angel.

2 Cut out the paper shapes and outline one body shape and two wings onto the cardboard. Mark where the holes go for the thread.

3 Cut out the cardboard wings and body.

4 Pierce the hole markings with a needle. ⊕

5 Color in the features on the wings and the angel body.

6 Using the needle and thread, sew the wings to the body.

7 Cut two long pieces of nylon thread and attach them to the outside holes in the wings and then to the piece of doweling.

8 Hold the doweling in the air and see the angel fly.

ENAMEL PAINTING

The folk art motifs used to paint these enamel mugs and plate are found on old enamel utensils all over the world. They are often done in bright colors on a strong black or green background. It's a good idea to do a practice painting on an old paint or candy tin.

What you need

old paint or sweet tin

sandpaper

paintbrushes

enamel paints

clear artist's varnish

thinner

1 To prepare the background, rub the metal down with a piece of sandpaper until it is smooth and clean.

2 Paint on two coats of background color and leave to dry.

3 Paint on a top coat and leave to dry.

6 Add a few dots and dashes for the flower centers. Leave to dry.

7 Finish with a coat of clear artist's varnish.

4 When painting your design, remember you are not trying to achieve a sophisticated look. Start by painting your background shapes for leaves and roses.

5 When your background shapes are dry, paint on the petal and leaf markings with single swift brushstrokes. Leave to dry.

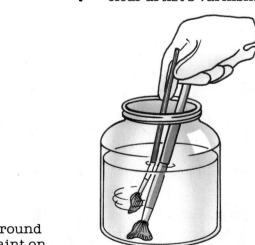

8 Wash the paintbrushes in thinner.

PAINTED CLOCKS

What you need

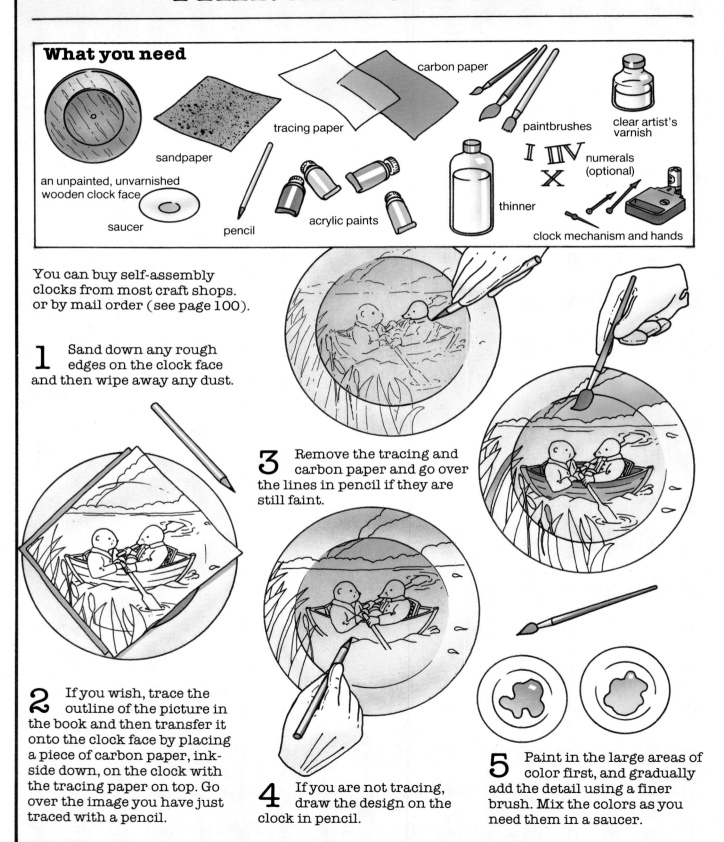

carbon paper

tracing paper

paintbrushes

clear artist's varnish

sandpaper

an unpainted, unvarnished wooden clock face

saucer

pencil

acrylic paints

thinner

numerals (optional)

clock mechanism and hands

You can buy self-assembly clocks from most craft shops. or by mail order (see page 100).

1 Sand down any rough edges on the clock face and then wipe away any dust.

2 If you wish, trace the outline of the picture in the book and then transfer it onto the clock face by placing a piece of carbon paper, ink-side down, on the clock with the tracing paper on top. Go over the image you have just traced with a pencil.

3 Remove the tracing and carbon paper and go over the lines in pencil if they are still faint.

4 If you are not tracing, draw the design on the clock in pencil.

5 Paint in the large areas of color first, and gradually add the detail using a finer brush. Mix the colors as you need them in a saucer.

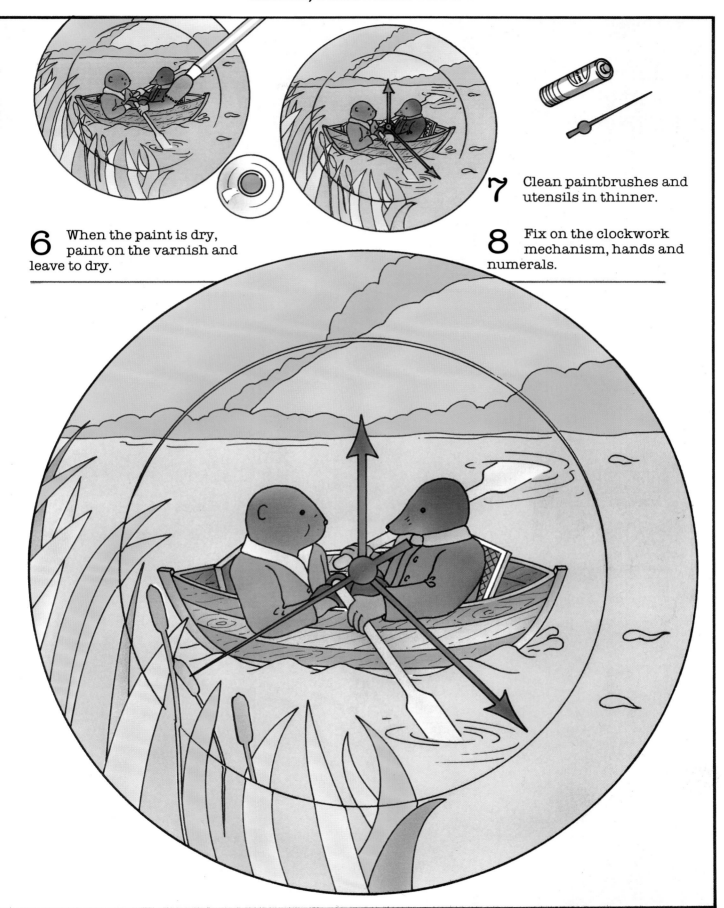

6 When the paint is dry, paint on the varnish and leave to dry.

7 Clean paintbrushes and utensils in thinner.

8 Fix on the clockwork mechanism, hands and numerals.

PAPER DECORATIONS

Here are some ideas for attractive decorations which can be made cheaply and easily at home.

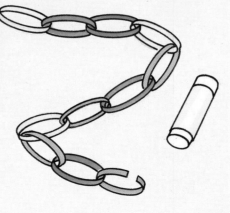

What you need

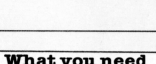

glue stick

strips of brightly colored paper (about 7in × 1in)

PAPER CHAIN

1 Glue the ends of the first strip together to form a ring, with the decorative side on the outside.

2 Thread the next strip through the first and glue the ends together.

3 Continue until the chain is the length you want it.

What you need

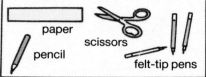

paper

pencil

scissors

felt-tip pens

PAPER DOLLS

1 Cut a strip of paper 14in long and 4in wide.

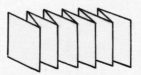

2 Fold the paper back and forth along the longest side into equal parts (about 2in) so it looks like a concertina.

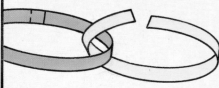

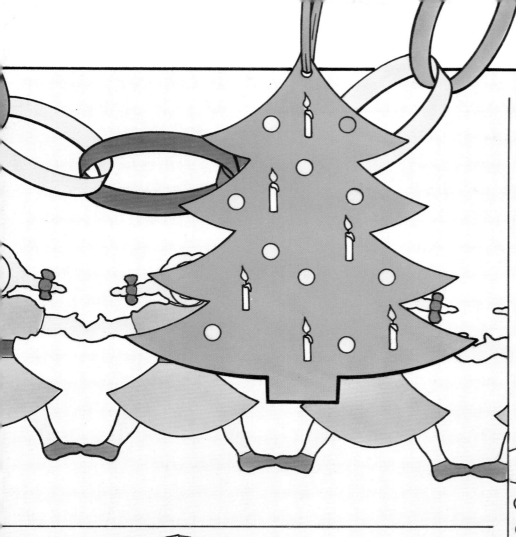

What you need

pencil

tracing paper   scissors

felt-tip pens

thin
cardboard

ribbon   hole punch

TREE DECORATIONS

1 Trace each shape in the book and cut out the traced patterns. Use these as your templates.

2 Place each template on the cardboard and draw around it in pencil.

3 Cut out the shapes.

4 Color in both the back and the front of each shape.

5 Punch a hole in the top of each shape, thread with ribbon and tie on a Christmas tree.

3 Draw the shape on the top of the folded paper, making sure the hands and feet of your doll are on the fold.

5 Open up the concertina to reveal a row of dolls.

4 Cut out the shape, making sure not to cut through the join.

6 Decorate with felt-tip pens.

97

MORE IDEAS

DECORATING PAPER WITH TEXTURES (pages 72—73)

There are endless ways of adding texture to paper with all sorts of different objects. Scrunch up a piece of paper or fabric. Dip it into paint and apply to a clean piece of paper. You could dab it, drag it or zigzag it to make different textures.

STENCILING (pages 74—77)

If you want to stencil on to a wall, floor or a piece of furniture, first ask permission! You can use stencil paints or emulsion or gloss paint. You will also need some thinner to wash your paintbrushes afterwards.

BROOCHES AND BADGES (pages 78—79)

Once you know how to make a brooch or a badge, you can decorate it in any way you like. You could make name badges for friends or write funny messages.

MARBLING PAPER (pages 82—83)

You can make very pretty paper by marbling. It can be used to make dollhouse wallpaper, wrapping paper, a cover for a book or to cover a matchbox to present a gift. You could also make greetings cards or your own writing paper.

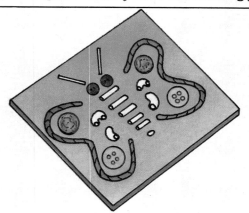

RUBBINGS (pages 80—81)

Making rubbings is one of the easiest ways to create patterns and textures. In addition to metal and stone, you can take a piece of paper and place it over any textured surface to make a rubbing with wax crayons. Try it on a brick wall, a tree trunk or a carved piece of wood. You can also make interesting rubbings from coins, doilies, string and even frosted glass.

MAKING AND USING BLOCKS (pages 84—85)

Try making a picture on a block of wood with string, pasta shapes, buttons and coins. Use the string as the outline of an animal and use the other materials to make the features and to decorate the background.

PAINTED CHINA (pages 86—87)

You can buy paints for glazed china which don't sink into the surface, so you can rub off your mistakes. Read the manufacturer's instructions carefully before using the paints.

Although they are durable, ceramic paints are best used for decoration rather than for objects which will be used every day.

Always have plenty of newspaper laid out on which to put the objects once they have been painted. Try to work in a dust-free room as ceramic paints pick up any fluff or particles from the air. Make sure you have plenty of thinner for diluting solvent-based paint and washing paintbrushes. Keep a couple of soft cloths by you: one dipped in thinner to wipe off mistakes and a dry one to wipe off any smears left by the wet one.

ANGEL MOBILE (pages 90—91)

As well as making an angel mobile, you could make a dragon, a flying horse or a pig with wings!

POP-UP CARDS (pages 88—89)

The lines that you cut out from the card to make a pop-up don't have to be horizontal. You could cut out the shape of a house or even an animal.

ENAMEL PAINTING (pages 92—93)

Once you have mastered enamel painting on an old tin can, try your hand at painting onto enamel mugs, plates, bowls or teapots. These can be bought in hardware stores. There is no need to sand the background down or to paint with three layers of enamel, unless you want to change the background color.

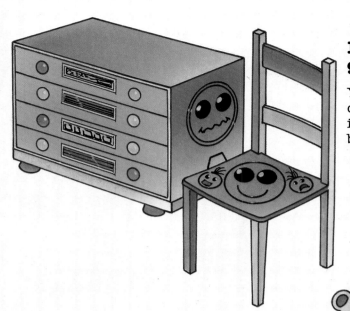

PAINTED CLOCKS (pages 94—95)

You can also decorate wooden chairs, chests of drawers or toy boxes. You could illustrate your favorite characters in a book or a film.

PAPER DECORATIONS (pages 96—97)

Paper dolls could be clowns, bears or gnomes. If you want to make really long rows, it is better to stick several short rows together, otherwise it becomes difficult to cut through the paper.

To cheer up your bedroom, cut balloons from large pieces of different-colored paper and stick them on the wall. Attach strips of ribbon to the bottom.

STOCKISTS AND ACKNOWLEDGEMENTS

The author would like to thank the following companies:

Euro Studio for supplying stencil blanks and brushes

Dylon International for supplying dyes and fabric pens

Self-assembly clocks are available by mail order from Panduro Hobby, West Way House, Transport Ave, Brentford, Middlesex.

Henkel Chemicals for supplying adhesives

3M for supplying tape

Art Graphic for supplying Pebeo fabric, ceramic and acrylic paints

Inscribe for supplying Fimo

INDEX